REPUBLIC

John, Una a Ifor Owen

REPUBLIC

Nerys Williams

Seren is the book imprint of
Poetry Wales Press Ltd.
Suite 6, 4 Derwen Road, Bridgend, Wales, CF31 1LH
www.serenbooks.com
facebook.com/SerenBooks
twitter@SerenBooks

ISBN: 9781781726969
Ebook: 9781781726976

A CIP record for this title is available from the British Library.

The publisher acknowledges the financial assistance of the Books Council of
Wales.

Cover artwork: Charles Uzzell-Edwards: 'Death Mask Blue'

Printed in Bembo by Severn, Gloucester

Contents

PREFACE

Republic in a Rule

These prose scatterings began from a need to commit an oral history to paper. Stories told, overheard, handed down, mostly in Welsh. It was no coincidence that this project began in 2015 in anticipation of the UK referendum. Many of the sections are attempts to sift through my relationship to Welsh. Some show how Welsh post-punk music enabled a love of language. Others attempt to understand what others make of linguistic difference. Some sections were written against a background of attacks made upon the Welsh language. It still seems that we are in a time when anything culturally different to an imagined "consensus" is presented as a drain on resources, or a threat.

I set myself a rule – each section was to be twenty sentences. The paragraph as a unit of thought; the sentence became a measure which enabled departures into *melos*, play, lyricism, sometimes humour. Rule-governed writing offers a paradoxical freedom. The format enabled writing to begin again, instances of completion became a closer possibility. Rules oddly generate chance, and associative word patterning make for narrative errancies.

And *Republic*? Perhaps it inscribes an experience of naturalisation into Irish citizenship and maybe the possibilities of a nation looking at itself from afar with (wry) independence.

1. Accordion

There are so many stories, the child lost count of how they came to be known. Some emerged from sweet wrappers, others from a box of fly-speckled birthday cards. One epic story came from an accordion. When the child pulled it from the case it let loose an almighty wheeze. Stories flew, mildewed, smelling of rot. The child tried to make the accordion sing. She told it – be *Tonic Sol-fa, make a pretty noise*. The buttons seized on cloth tapered underneath. Hoisting the leather straps on her shoulders, angry sounds tumbled to her feet. The accordion is dark blue inlaid with mother of pearl. It is the body of horrible sound. Worse were the sweet spores as it moved in and out. The breath of a dead man encased in a trapezium coffin.

A teacher told them of a poet who described breath. The poet had been accused of using too many words to explain simple things. He made a wheeze so large it became monstrous. The noise brought up her grandmother from the shop below, who quietly said "put it away". The accordion was battling for breath, the bellows refused to close. However much the child squeezed the leather clasp, it would not shut. She wedged the box between the wall and a table, hoping it would be silent.

2. Gwynfor

Writing against music I try to find the momentum of days. The sound of a political poster being unfurled and put into my hands. I could be three, could be four. The banner is neon green and reads *Gwynfor*. I am smiling, is it from understanding or looking to the background? I am held on either side by parental hands. Look they say this is you. This is what it is to know a language that is presently dying. This is the language that we use, that we speak when we put on the immersion, unpack our Christmas presents. This is the language we use when sorting out clothing on the line. This is the language that tells me what I have done wrong. This is the language hummed at night. Later, I would know Gwynfor as a man who was prepared to go on hunger strike. But for the moment, Gwynfor is the man with the benign smile thanking me for reciting a poem about a small boy and a stinking fish, during a political benefit night. I have memorised the poem and feel smart in my black and white striped rayon dress with its pussy bow. The poem is humorous, but I am thrown when adults laugh at the punch line. Did I do wrong? "Make sure that you own the stage" my father whispers. "Don't start until everything is quiet. Own the stage."

3. Anti-Memoirist

It has to be of the place. It has to retain movement, not be nostalgic or indulgent. It has to write itself, the process of making. Whether that might be the taste of orange spilt on the chin, or explosive coke cans showering children in the back of the bus. It has to tell the truth about speaking a language that is constantly under threat, first from its own people, then the quangos and finally by a lack of conviction and hurt. It has to tell more than a story of an individual, a community, not the saccharine loss found in mediocre memoirs. It has to tell of the feathery feeling that once met as life, becomes love. It has to tell of the small vial of tears that you keep on a shelf, its cut glass catches the sun. It has to tell the story of oil and sweat, and broken-down things repaired, remastered then sold. This might be the story of smoke, how smoke curls into the lungs to be blown into punctuation marks in the sky. This might be the story of small things becoming bigger and punctured by a lack of insight. This might be the story of an old record player that crackles, it is painted a deep blue, its speakers drop in and out. The music becomes a background noise of feed in and feedback.

Can you complete the loop of a disturbed song? This might be the telling of more than one life, how lives intersect, are borrowed, are tried on like mothballed fur coats (in boxes on cupboards). This might be the big strip tease, a series of a life in objects. The pen you found on a dresser. The woman with a swimsuit once turned, her breasts slip out as the ink slides down. The woman's expression is the same, a forced smile of tedium. Please dear reader, let this not be me.

4. Innovation

They put you in a little box called innovative. To *innovate* (with no object attached): *Make changes in something established, especially by introducing new methods, ideas, or products* – "the company's failure to diversify and innovate competitively." Was I in a company or *in* company? Is this what I am writing in these sections: a book of lies about innovation?

Some expressed the view that fewer and fewer employers are willing to take risks with ideas or to innovate. Or, maybe to innovate with an object such as *Introduce (something new, especially a product): we continue to innovate new products.* She bit her pen and thought, whenever the word "innovative" had been applied it meant difficult to sell, or market.

What we need is a story telling us something we already know. Preferably nothing to do with a minority language, that is so uncool. Maybe rhyme a little more, at the very least punctuate, don't be too sonic. Weren't minority languages innovative since they were constantly adapting to market forces, the ones that survived did. Or, could they be harnessed to technology?

The drive to constantly innovate product and process is strongly visible. Mid 16th century: *from Latin innovate – renewed, altered, from the verb innovare, from in- into + novare make new (from novus "new").* She wasn't new, she just felt old, wearing her charity shop polyester, too snug around her chest. Maybe she should adopt a bilingual avatar and write macaronically. She was reminded of a stern, but wise American poet she once met for coffee. He advised her to read the poetry that will keep you sane, the textual communities that take you away from bureaucracy; *making new* was not about the last best new thing in the review section. Indeed, according to some, making new never existed anyhow, unoriginal genius is where it is at. Can the writer ever be a catalyst for change?

5. Teacher

The day she heard of the accident something broke. There was no evidence, no splinter under a nail, no bruising. There was talk in the corridors that her favourite teacher's car was found flung against a tree on a bent road. They said she no longer knew the opening lines to *Macbeth*, that her husband was in the hospital waiting for her to wake. Nobody knew if she had language. Her son pallid, his heartbreaker looks assumed a flash of hardness. He was the first boy she had known to cover his love bites with plasters. On prize giving day he walked onto the stage and grinned knowingly. That first day, her dramatic entrance of boots, a blonde bob and russet suede skirt, we read a poem about a foxhunting man who was no more.

You were the only one that knew the word "quince", a miniature bush in front of your bungalow. The teacher had looked disapprovingly when you were caught speaking softly with a boy in the English room, holding hands. "*Gainst the powers of evil our arms are assailing*"- cried the choir in the teacher's production "Out, Out, Brief Candle". The choir used pillowslips as tunics, sprayed with car paint, black suns with gold rays. Girls with breasts had to run their own costumes. All sang of evil and redemption. The production needed tights with mother smells, the rags that covered witches as they spat on stage. *Strongest earthly night must be unavailing*; girls sniggered at Lady Macbeth's soliloquies; the boys looked at her chest. Entrances and exits timed to harpsichord and acapella. Words were portals, the spotlight beat us blind and breathing. You believed *we are a composite of those we've loved and the words we've read*.

6. Not your Music, But my Making.

Somebody comments on the albums you love with authority. Tarnishing the grooves of vinyl. You've played this game, observed the right amount of vintage set against the right amount of eyeliner framed with the "new". Anti-fashion was DIY in your small town. Farmers' wives disposed of their psychedelia, vinyl red macs, and cotton dresses. Time spent threading needles, bloodying your fingers and palm while you refashion a suede coat.

Easier was the dyeing of 1950s aprons, cutting them into new dresses. Working into the night, delightedly hand sewing hems and replacing buttons. Same template each time taken from a *Miss Selfridge* shift dress, marked up crudely and cut out. There had to be proper dance shoes – for pogo jumping, stamping on plastic beer glasses that split against black tights.

But where is the music in this? Illegal taping, the decoupage covers of mix tapes. Adverts in fanzines and the Welsh mag *Brych ap Collwyn ap Tango* – afterbirth with its telescoping title of "ap". Politics and music merged seamlessly, you always found it strange when asked, how does music become political? Language surely made music political. Having no vocabulary yet to speak of your linguistic life. Sending away for seven-inch compilations whose keyboards parodied pop, the bass strung to heartbeat. Starting from disco, you jettison feathers, sequins and glitter, sliding your feet into the imprint of used army boots. Growing your fringe over your eyes, jumping like a boy. Crashing, contorting your body at angles, forgetting your growing breasts.

7. The Perruque

That second before they re-enter your life. Anticipating the voice of the small child speaking to your husband. You have inhabited this space, welcoming the return but also resistant to leave thought's measure. You are afraid of being caught, the perversity of not doing what one is tasked to do. There is the pull of practical tasks, diversions, necessary but pleasurable things.

At fifteen you searched for a picture frame for your Bogart print bought on a school exchange in Brittany. A week in October cold with a trench coat and brown brogues that pinched your feet. You thought that your French exchange student understood. Most of her English was focussed on the rendition of power ballads in an American accent. This was years before you encountered a connective with Belmondo in *Breathless*. Returned, you found a frame, a black and white picture of your mother being handed something by a woman with a handbag and a hat. Your mother young, the picture official, but the frame suited Bogart's face so you decided to place him over your mother. The frame was a dull brown, in the garage you found the metallic green your father and uncle used to remodel the right wing of the Chrysler Sunbeam. The new hatchback car, on your birthday your mother reversed into a lorry smashing the rear window. The remains of shattered windscreen glass, small remnants left under a tree, kids saw the accident. Your birthday but your focus was on your mother's puffy face. Years later your father and uncle would cut the rusted wing, replace the hole with mesh and filler, sculp it and spray it acidic green. You find the can and spray the photo frame. Humphrey Bogart covers the photo of your mother as young nurse receiving her award for leadership. You didn't realise its importance until the photo could not be found.

8. Come Together (for Geiger)

"Recall the 1980s in the small town, don't wax lyrical about music the making of dresses, the eyeliner on the boys you love." There were strikes, protests, *When the Wind Blows, Z for Zachariah,* "Two Tribes" a nuclear bunker built by the council. A woman lost her finger on the fence protesting the half-made bunker, everybody wore CND badges, older sisters went to Greenham for the weekend. Anti-nuclear protestors made friends with the peace people, the religious people made friends with the peace people too. The Welsh language protestors made friends with everybody, since all wanted the world to breathe more easily.

The bunker features in an undercover history of Wales. A manhole in a carpark, metal rungs to the control room, the camera lingers on a shelf of broken A4 folders, two feet of water. You cannot see any Welsh signage – how quickly the technology of loudspeakers and control panel ages, the bunks are rusty. You wonder if they had a Geiger counter and which councillor would operate it. The only councillor prepared to defend the bunker (live on S4C) was a family friend. You did not see the programme but glean a narrative from overheard adult conversations. A discussion about radioactivity and water after fallout, your grandmother's praise "those CND types are educated, they were having none of it." The councillor said he had his own well water. Which brought catcalls of "I'm alright Jack" from the panellists expert in half-lives, poisoning and carbon 14. Before Chernobyl. Your childhood was about fighting for things, banners and placards, adults circling a carpark. A satirical Welsh pop song about Margaret Thatcher: *Let the unemployed move to Kent and get a job.* Elfyn Presli shouting "Thatcher's Jackboots" into a mic, fascism was royal blue and bouffanted. The sad-eyed councillor came to pick up groceries at night, you were tempted to draw a CND circle on his muddied car. Pausing, you pictured the heat of studio lights, his failing language, moved away from the bonnet knowing the battle was won.

9. Work Experience

Suddenly there is work, the need to prove oneself possible of work in West Wales of the 1980s. The school decided that they were having "work experience"; serving petrol, cutting cheese and decanting paraffin at a grandmother's shop, did not count. Work is a vocational path, a career, except the daughter did not know what she wanted to do except read more books and make small dresses out of bigger dresses while sipping whiskey listening to the *Modern Jazz Quartet*.

You see the daughter had a romantic idea of how an "anti-career" might look. The teacher was a despot, he militarised everything, his notes, ties, even his socks. Small pickings in 1980's West Wales, Thatcher made sure of that. My West was permanent home for tourists, arms testing as well as reintroducing the red kite. What was there for a sixteen year-old looking for work experience?

Some went to see veterinarians castrating kittens, others haunted the offices of small town lawyers, another helped out a hairdresser with spiral perms. She blow-dried a client's hair to a frazzle, looking in the mirror, wondering whether she needed to lose weight before she bought a pair of leather trousers. One friend worked in a bookshop, continued reading while scorning the owner's advances. Another hung around the office of a small town newspaper waiting to attend funerals and the opening of a new supermarket. The daughter knew she needed to get away from the veterinarian, the surgeries, the lawyer's office and the advertising copy of small town journalism. She wanted "experience" to mean getting on trains, sitting in cafes and finding out more about music and life.

She remembered a magazine she'd picked up in the closest city. Its typeface shouted a name *IMPACT*. The city had been bombed during the second world war, civic pride now entailed concrete subways, walkways and hanging baskets. She liked this city with its cheap second-hand clothing, its quadrant of bright plastic facias, and its *Kardomah* café named after the café frequented by a painters, artists and poets, atomised during the war. She liked the magazine's profiles of alternative bands and photoshoots set in industrial estates and abandoned government buildings. Hungry for an experience of "getting somewhere."

10. Editing

It is difficult knowing what to do in an office. She sat on the floor in her dungarees reading *The Catcher in the Rye* waiting for the editor. The building next door was a print works and offices for *THE ECHO and EVENING POST*. She did not like the novel, it felt alien to a daughter living in the country with no skyscrapers and subways. Not that literature (she reasoned) had to be set in her own landscape for her to feel affinity, it was also tedious. The editor came, soft spoken, hair falling into his eyes, "I had forgotten about Holden Caulfield, Come in." The small room smelt of glue, paper and coffee. The daughter was shy and did not know what kind of work she might do. But the editor was kind and asked her to file the stills cabinet. Opening the first drawer she gasped, stills from the films at her local *Lyric*: *The Mission, Platoon, A Room with a View, Fatal Attraction, Absolute Beginners*. Touching these surfaces was a communion with film. Before downloadable images their reading involved their holding, a tactile thing. Conversation at first was slight, they started exchanging band names, book titles, place names and favourite foods. The editor, a practicing Buddhist, found it strange selling products that readers did not need. The daughter argued that there was art there too. Particularly in the new front cover: a model with peroxide hair, poised like Grace Jones on *Island Life* wearing a pink tutu, two spiral cut coke cans for a bra. "The reviews" she said "don't forget new music and books." The editor smiled, picking a skein of glue from his tapering fingers after a night of putting the magazine to bed. He shook his head "The reviews are the worst." David Byrne in the background asking: *Psycho Killer Quest-ce que c'est?*

11. Imprint

for Mandy Jackson and Jon Ashwell

I can't give everything... I can't give everything — away. It might be that this daughter spent her time partying in heels, making for a tight spine later in life. It might be that the prodigal daughter bought herself a skull-print scarf before such scarves became commonplace.

I once knew a bright-bold daughter who was no prodigal. She worked next door to a magazine in the city which was close enough to the country and the sea. The bright-bold daughter held a Prince of Wales award and her office shocked when you first entered. There were shelves of teeth, set in plaster, she called them *her gnashers*. I wondered what it was like to work with so many dental impressions, grinning clenched. We'd cradle tea the three of us, me shy, the editor and the bright-bold daughter: her hair bleached, eyes framed by blue mascara, purple eye shadow.

I pictured her leaving the vast building at night, its rattling metal banister, broken service lifts and mesh fencing. The teeth would chatter, speaking, no tongues. Gapped front teeth whistling for attention, the loose-jawed testing words against a hard palette, nipping invisible lips. At dawn, silence. Those late spring afternoons, heat in the palm of one's hand, listening to the bright-bold daughter — she'd almost lost the teeth to a gust of wind. The dental imprints had shuddered, shoving one another to the brink. Later that summer, the editor sent me a letter care of school. The bold bright daughter had been set alight by her ex, he watched her burn like a candle. The editor felt lonely without her, he missed her crooked smile, the cups of tea that broke long afternoons typesetting. It was the first time somebody you knew died on TV, a story on the national news. You smelt the petrol and willed a whisper: "I do not dream, I am not afraid of anything anymore."

12. No Future

The time came for the young woman to think of a future: she thought of university as something far away; typed out enquires for prospectuses on a manual typewriter bought at a local fundraiser. *University* suggested formality, she would need to prove her commitment to this process through typing everything (badly).

Nobody in her family knew about universities. The only careers lesson she could remember was a video about a young man going to a London bedsit with an orange rucksack, he warmed beans on a camping stove. It was unsaid, but the fate of this young man was sealed; as he fastidiously spooned his food on a plate she imagined prostitution and snuff videos. There were sniggers in the room when the tape stuck, the adviser (he was a woodwork teacher – *Psychedelic Hits* in his car) barked "What do you want from this class." A brave voice answered, "more information." "What kind?"' he asked exasperated, she replied, "how to sign on" the class laughed again. This was not meant to be funny; she had grown up with "1 in 10", the Miners' strike, milk quota protests, the privatisation of gas and telephone and soon to be water and electricity. Also *Z for Zachariah* and a touring theatre group about heroin junkies, a *just say no* production which included simulated vomit. She'd seen her uncle return from a failing marriage, chain-smoking, broken and living at home, his mother paying his bus driver's licence which had elapsed, he only had the money for the Severn crossing in his pocket. Fear of the apocalyptic and protests over jobs had coalesced into an abstract space pulsing with the Pistols' "God Save the Queen" and The Cure's "The Top".

Her parents thought it best to talk to a genius family friend, as a teenager he stayed in bed chewing matches and devouring books. His life had been idiosyncratic, he put dirt in his school sandwiches and had disassembled an engine on the sheets of his bed. Sitting his 'A-Levels' twice for fun, since he was too young to start a medical degree in London, he became a heavy drinker. She admired this man who spoke aphoristically, he'd returned to the small community without a degree and quietly settled into lab work. His advice was to gesture to a prospectus of "dreaming spires", but she doesn't understand its dense writing, the references to periods of literary study so remote from her love of Camus and de Beauvoir. Besides, she already fought her English teacher in scholarship class and slammed the door hard. When it came to her interviews another family friend said "wear a hat and gloves"; even she of no-university knowledge knew times had changed.

13. Fangirl

Today she walked Berkeley while listening to my bloody valentine's *loveless*. She's yet to hear of psychogeography, but tries crossing streets to the feedback of Kevin Shields's guitar. Dazzling strangeness, her boots kick against a sidewalk thrown up by tree roots, sun touching face and throat. A breeze as she canters to class, Shakespeare (in Northern California). A student stands up raising a hand but falls bouncing against the stools. The crowd circles, the professor kneels to help, Joy Division moves into her mind *lost control again*. The student is OK and later would thank the group in the next lecture, shyly remarking *Julius Caesar* would never be the same.

Her experiment: can mbv's "soon" frame the time it takes to walk from campus to her apartment? Past hummingbirds, a Bernard Maybeck church with its porch of sleeping bodies, wisteria and notched wood on Bowditch. She could go down Telegraph and try a smile, people are hurting and need change. Her roommate works as a house painter (no insurance) and leaves dollar bills near sleeping bags in early morning cold *can't get used to this*. Cody's the first book shop with a wall of poet portraits. She tried enacting a scene from *The Graduate,* drinking earl grey tea on the balcony in *Caffe Mediterraneum* —a group of men, dogs and trollies outside. Pretending to be a writer but not convinced by the observations in a notebook, which are mechanical and absurd. "I am a woman from a small, no record shop town tracing a recording of sidewalks through sound", the tape flips over to "only shallow".

Years later she finds out that Shields played all the guitars for the recording of *loveless* – he trusted nobody. When it came to performing live, the band were terrified. *The Warfield* in San Francisco on the 3rd July 1992 she watched the effects pedals as my bloody valentine closed with "You made me realise". The morning after a radio presenter asks her over the phone in Welsh whether she had seen any stars in California. Ears still buzzing with feedback, she could only mumble *Bilinda and Kevin,* disappointing the nation terribly.

14. Womanwords

We joined the film society wearing a uniform of Dr. Martens and stripy shirts. Membership included discussions about production values, camera angles and the refusal to offer an ending. We counted during *Drowning by Numbers* and delayed time with *The Magnificent Ambersons.* Now we are closer to Jeanne Moreau's age in *The Immortal Story.* We always want to be lit by candlelight; Welles directed that scene with the sailor so lovingly. Poor Falstaff as he tumbles into the *Chimes at Midnight* with a foppery of followers. We embraced the industrial, our shoes indented with metal strips. One stripped her mother's midwifery case down to its steel core and was promptly ejected from the library for her detector-proof bag. The metal case was cold when it snowed, it rattled into lectures, making people stare – *exhibitionist.* Some would never finish as film students. One friend filmed another in her short *The Curse,* which dramatised a first period. No special effects only a yellow nightshirt and a pool of red paint. Her second film used *Womanwords: A Dictionary of Words About Women* (1991). Just to be clear, this was not *Communicating Gender, Beyond Language Power and the Classroom, The Psychology of Women and Work* or even *Cunt: A Declaration of Independence.* All these come later, but revenge is always sweet. The voiceover was performed by a professor, beady-eyed he had followed her throughout second year. He professed himself a Jungian telling the class that recording his dreams caused his divorce. The premise was basic, she shot campus footage: women walking back and forth past fountains, into class, eating, talking, thinking. She recorded the Jungian whispering woman words: *Hips, legs, mouth, breast, slip, scent.* Forcing him to listen to himself in the editing suite.

15. Bring back British Leyland

You think that if you listen to Ludovico Einaudi it might make things seem a little better. His music underscores the most unlikely of programmes. Some time ago the album had been sent to you by a beloved friend, who unknown to you was dying. *Una Mattina* – you listened and thought of your friend's hands at the piano with a hammered gold ring on his left pinkie. The music played since giving up performing. Tired of pop covers in bars he preferred a small audience at his baby grand. He was not looking for international success.

Einaudi began appearing in the substrata of radio features, a shorthand to a poignant moment, becoming a symbol of nostalgia, awareness, breath, spots of time. So popular now you feared that it was a sonic wallpaper. His music as counterpoint to skinhead culture in *This is England*. *Fuori Dal Mondo* not of this world, *Nuvole Bianche* white clouds, which move us so far from the cement and spray paint of Thatcher's jackboots. Or, does it punctuate the brutal beauty of that time? Kicking against nostalgia, keep calm, democracy exercised in public school debates? Is nostalgia an exercise that can only be entertained by the affluent? The poor buy a cheaper present. What does it mean for politics to trade in nostalgia? Retrofitting ourselves, inserting adjectives into names, repeating ourselves in the process. A constitutional conversation which never takes place in public. Buy the present, fix the future. Bring back British Leyland.

16. Unfriend me

Social media documents your waking dream. A lost narrative of the world: the constant hum, white noise, electrical pulse, the zeitgeist moves away once more.

Those you sought to ignore now follow you, assert daily tastes, their likes, people love to collect other people. You would rather not feel their social breathing. Space that once was a form of reasoning, a filter for information in the world, now a moving PR campaign. Are you being petulant? Is there a moment of grief in this story?

Take for example the best friend you knew when pop was made of dipped fringes, you loved her moodiness, leather gloves and thoughtfulness. You loved her parents, the father who read the Quran because he was curious (before Iraq, before Afghanistan). The beautiful mother dying too young, she wanted you to remain best friends. But your friend married a man who slapped her bottom in public, told her when to finish telephone conversations. Having less in common, the giggling days of eyeliner were replaced with lists to fulfil the man.

The true friend became demanding, texting during the night, "please reply", you were never fast enough, not *there* enough. She did not understand your commute between countries or your hopeless affairs. Could you ever repair a friendship that had run out of will and intimacy? Angry letters and texts, a position of systematic withdrawal. Until in desperation, your friend praised your poem on the search for a child, not understanding how social media worked. Poor friend humiliated in public. All you could think about was how she travelled six thousand miles with your grandmother's pound cake in her hand luggage, through all those security scans. Bringing sweet mouthfuls to California twenty five years ago, tasting love.

17. Learning what your problem is

In the Californian morning, there is insistence in the robin's two beat song, she sits on a stone bench reading. It is the longest poem telling of selfhood, dirt, ownership. It smears language on lips, teeth, desire at its core. Though it is chilly, she sits in a blue gingham dress, reading forward, then flicking back. One army boot kicks rhythmically, she moves through pronouns, cradling her coffee cup for warmth. West Wales to the West Coast. Under the sight of the campanile her study has become aspirational.

Her dear friend the jazz pianist wrote before interview: "Go get, America". Except there have been breakages, curfews, returning to the footage of Rodney King bludgeoned in LA, "Fascism" sprayed on campus walls. On the phone she answers her friend's question from DC - *what is this curfew about?* King on the news, she sat on the floor, getting groceries during the day, hearing the helicopters circling. Sirens a block away. A poet in his lecture on Laurence Dunbar discussed the sickening attack, and cried. The only time she heard a professor become so intimate was when a bearded man told them they might enter university working class, but would leave their education middle class.

Confusion that first semester, had she had taken a wrong turn? This new pedagogue made poetry a visceral thing, less an abstract fluttering than a tractable metal shaping mind's flight. He ventriloquised what one might be able to hear. How access to learning is an issue of race, class, economics, and debt. How white her classroom was when he spoke of King. Would you or they, ever truthfully address your relationship to what Claudia Rankine & Beth Loffreda call out as the *racial imaginary*?

18. Superglue

Having a crush is mesmerizing, an illness, memorialising encounters. Staring in the mirror half-smiling. Its attractive impossibility. That nothing happens is a key pleasure. One wills the beloved into being, walking across the street, you hold your head to avoid it tumbling. A thought-cloud which might disclose its full frames of reference. A scarlet pain, it fills the head and heart with shame. Do I own the crush, or does the crush own me?

It might be the making of a gesture, the holding of one's chin, the satisfaction of admiring the way a beloved walks, smiles, or touches the side of their face thinking. And how to disguise it? Never tell your friend. Avoid your crush with friends, they will make you wince with self-consciousness. Never take a big-mouthed Yorkshire man to a poetry reading. He will draw attention, refusing to pay, eating all the artful *hors d'oeuvres* and speak loudly about the frail, anxious listeners. The delicate sensibility of the crush bearer, willing other worlds into being.

You go to a thrift store and buy a red dress with a flurry of scalloped layers, it reminds you of Frida Kahlo and Diego Rivera in canvas. You might accessorise this dress with army boots and a rucksack. There might be the desire to perform your curious hybrid: breathing in Welsh speaking English. Because of poetry, you take a broken violin case and make a H.D. memorial, a bricolage of dried grasses, seashells, spent pesos. Superglued also is a mirror with three dead wasps nestling into a dried rose.

19. Rememory

I am lost in the contorted image of a pub. I scroll back to the pedestrian image but cannot get away from a couple who have ordered their dinner and are waiting. Faces pixelated, seated at a polished table. Thankfully I see the emergency exit. My cursor and I stumble down the patterned carpet step, finally to air and traffic.

I have been "home" already, though home is a walk from my ex-boyfriend's house near a cathedral graveyard. I never noticed that we had a back gate, it was rarely warm enough to hang our washing. Bell practice every Wednesday night, even with closed shutters, ear plugs, trying to enter Californian poetry for its last glimmer of warmth – discordant knells punctuated words. Naming the plants I never saw: Meadowsweet, Queen Anne's Lace, Morning glory. Winter's dazzling days, snow on the morning street. Marrow-cold in a house with only a small gas fire, cotton duvets, sheeted ice, socks in bed. Desperate for a taste of sun, the philosopher and I bought avocados, mashed them, added lemon and salt, turned up the heater. Our knitted-selves toasted dappled light with each dip.

Memories of my younger self often circle gatherings at modest feasts. Follow the cursor to a café filled with coffee, panettone and ice cream, orange, pink and green sweet boxes stacked on the shelves. Or, do I turn the corner to find my student-self? Encountering a stalker past bushes and winding river, I ran home breathless, sick. The night of celebrating scholarships to the US the philosopher, filmmaker and I were manifesto making. A night imagining passage on a liner, careering to Sinatra, romanticising ourselves in steerage. The figure at my heels gaining the measure of my two-step, three-step, four-step five-step, six, seven, eight...

20. Reading in Private

What is privacy, does the self-implode if serenaded too long? I wanted the default, the misremembered, the error of losing, a work that harboured deceit.

Once upon a time there was a girl and a boy who met when they were eighteen. Friends for three years before becoming lovers. Scared of shredding the unspoken. The friendship circled study, records and film, he dared not touch her. One night after she left the party in the small apartment he kicked a partition wall. Only in the final year of their study did they begin. Starting with a look, a touch in a small cottage listening to sonic guitars. An album that brought them back to their journeying. A touch so slight, arms brushing against one another to become holding, hugging, kissing. Desperate happiness in finally *being there* with no outside. *Love in a hut with water and a crust, Is Love, forgive us! – cinders, ashes, dust.*

A pattern of work and days the problems of finding a living, her head burst with reading, he asked her to move in. Now fearing the unspoken, bracing herself for hurt, she found his diary. A flat in the Gorbals, his hands hard from hammering rental signs high above the city. She found an entry written to another woman "you are the sultana in my chickpea curry" followed by a thought of their relationship "It will be X's birthday, does she wait to hear from me, I miss her." The guilt of reading palpable. But her eye caught another entry. "I still feel bad that time I found her diary while she was travelling, I read it to understand her."

21. Community

Always firelight in the house, for boiling water and drying clothes, childhood was a movement between stifling heat and extreme cold. In woollen socks, several blankets on the bed, scraping the ice from inside windows. Bags of granulated sugar moved from the shop to the airing cupboard, sharing space with coats. Mice leave teeth marks, cocooned winter to spring; during summer uninhabitable spaces open. Detergent, the petrol pump's motor, my grandmother's laugh at some customer's joke.

Those summers I stretched in the bed above, reading. The concrete and small pebbled shop floor mopped and covered with newspapers. A fly's buzz in summer morning, windows in the dark interiors of stone thick-walled buildings. Yellow plastic bowl serving as a till, suede black bag, serves as a bank. The bag carried each night up steep stairs, placed under the bed. Contents counted with the kitchen door locked and curtains closed. Your grandmother orders the notes, you the coins into neat piles, to buy the next delivery of petrol. "If we have a thousand you choose a treat from the shop" we are always over.

Boxes which offer such possibilities: a house/horse/boat/broken and burnt near the river. You want castor oil from the 60s, Keller's butterscotch, looped sanitary towels, small plastic combs that slip easily into a side pocket? Cheese sits on a slab in the cold of the shop, sweet as a nut. For the woman who lives in the longhouse under the brow of a hill there are petit fours, heaven in dusted pink and yellow. In the counter drawers that that never shut. You smell *DRUM* shag, *GOLDEN VIRGINIA, LAMBERT & BUTLER* cigarettes next to gold boxes of *BENSON & HEDGES*. Now when you shop for images, typefaces inscribed with a pastness that shocks, moving you into nostalgia.

22. London Welsh

London does not seem so far anymore. In 1963 a young woman goes to London from a village in West Wales to train as a nurse. She hates it for the first nine months, writing home she hopes the hospital will fall *brick by brick.*

From those first weeks she recalls drudgery and medical hierarchies. Her first task was to make a big pail of porridge. During this time the hospital advances with radical experiments in heart bypass surgery. By the age of 22 she researches an article, a case study, it is published in a medical journal. You encounter her homesickness, letters sealed in a tartan tin, her mother wrote every week. Sick for language, moved from a valley to blackened brick.

Photos tell you she learned sophistication quickly. Her chubby faced shyness changes to the figure of a woman who accessorises. She attends a wedding in a navy dress coat, an orange hat sculpted like a helmet on her head. You ask her about the sixties, dismayed by her record collection with a "Help!" 7 inch and *Val Doonican Rocks, but Gently**. The LP cupboard is full with Welsh language trios and male voice choirs of the London Welsh. Once she saw The Rolling Stones at the Palladium but was unimpressed, nurses were given spare tickets. Theatres offered caseworkers opportunities they could not afford. Pay was slight, her first friend left gnawed by homesickness. Your mother saved all her money for return journeys home. Travel with trunks and carriages, sliding doors, smoke in tunnels, the locomotive was slow. She patted the train each time, adding "thank you".

---

* On 31st December 1967 Val Doonican's album replaced The Beatles' *Sgt. Pepper's Lonely Hearts Club Band* from no1 position in the UK album chart

23. Listening

A time of open season on anything different, if you dressed differently, spoke differently to what was "expected". This was the time of homogeneity and "England" was as mystifying as it was unapproachable, a monument in the mind of others.

Your language drains our resources, ruins our businesses, fills our supermarkets with bilingual nouns, the insistence of Welsh first on your signage. Yes, indeed sir/madam I nearly crashed the car on that roundabout. In short, you are an anarchist language which threatens my possibility of a) getting a job b) getting money for the services I demand c) achieving a worthwhile and idyllic monolingual life ch) sanity, your language talks about me. Did I just enter ch) instead of d) see you have infiltrated my alphabet? I wanted to write a volume that was a) not nostalgic b) offered a document in its time c) would make people understand.

In short, I was hoping for the magic of C.D. Wright and listened to her interviews while writing, hoping something might enter, a sense of responsiveness. To fill in the time delay between perception and its evocation, listening and its resounding. More than anything listening was the agency I craved most. As a philosopher once said that to listen "will always then, to be straining toward an approach to the self." The philosopher adds once one is listening "one is on the lookout for a subject, something (itself) that identifies itself by resonating from self to self." I am at ground zero in this argument, having to explain what it is to live *in* a language. Our language that shyly reverberates and shines yet is questioned by @newsnight @sportsdirect: can we afford your language, are you not harbouring terrorism? I taste the word *diaspora* willing Welsh speakers in the world descend on the institutions that treat them shabbily, holding their Mr Urdd Gonks, waving placards in red paint, singing primary school songs and generally being a nuisance in the Welsh language.

I will that "listening" becomes a signature to a movement of thinking, an attempt to exceed the self. To overcome images which mean more than poor Tom Jones licking the last resonance of "Delilah". I will that our language becomes a buzzing in the ears of the tribe. The six year old in me who looked in disbelief as the Royal cavalcade sped through our small town. We were marched early that jubilee morning, waving union jacks, a friend thought we saw somebody raise a pale hand.

24. 1989

I live in a village made of different of architectural styles: arcades, cornices, colonnades, entablatures, turrets, trusses and rotundas. All harnessed into new structures, brokered into reimagining. Houses and clock towers painted yellow, pink, orange and white fixed with aquamarine metal stairs, shutters and railings. A temple holds a gold plaster Buddha from a film set, in winter a scarf round his neck, brightening the dark. In the dream, stones are gradually unpainted, the cornices and colonnades gyrate, and fly, trusses and rotundas blown into the sky. Stones roll down the small hill into the sea. Slate creaks under the wind scratching against wood, spiralling, called back into scars of filleted quarries. Architectural salvage returned: the 18th century ceiling with its scenes of Herculean tasks searches for its mansion home. The mansion gone, demolished.

Do you mock these reconstructions as a paean to postmodernism, thwarting stable signifiers? Mountain to sea, cornice to scree, the small glint of the swimming pool from the crow's eye. Robin's egg blue to darkest cobalt. Sky reflected in a body of water. The surprise of an empty swimming pool, leaves in its corners, small hard apples. Those final hours before weeks of exams, searching for passage to another form of life, tracing the slope and depth of the school swimming pool. Gifted to the girl's grammar school (before it became Welsh comprehensive) your mother bobbed in this same space during the 1950s. These last days, the class of 1989, friends lie on its empty floor in perpendicular poses. Emulating The Monkees in summer dresses, a burst of The Primitives on the cassette deck. You tried to customise those uniforms, pulling in, taking up, finding 70s sandals with block heels, challenging starched fabrics and tough buttons. The gift now filled in and tarmacked, a car park for council administrators.

25. Performance

There comes in your 30s the urgent need to... Become a rock star, a performing poet, a somebody who can handle a wardrobe, speak to crowds without falling prey to your own ego. It is an indescribable need, not for fame, but the need for something that exceeds the self. You always associate exceeding with Levinas' words and this awareness as altruism. You see this "exceeding" all around you, dormant in the lives of women who have played it right, worked the rules, conscientiously filed the documents. Then POW, they want to become rock stars. They want to play bass like Kim Gordon, bare legged in a long striped t-shirt. They want to smile beatifically into space like Kim Deal interjecting "Your bone's got a little machine". They want to be held in ultramarine and fuchsia light and scale the octaves like Elizabeth Fraser. They dream of contorting their stiff bodies into a playful touching of fingers against lips, then scream as if Bjork was their voice coach. Or, looking into the future, slide into noise with Bilinda Butcher and no earplugs.

This sound in your heart, makes it difficult to attend meetings, look at spreadsheets, write references, fill in applications for funding, answer questionnaires on how infrastructures are helping/ loving / killing the "power" of literature. Young women that come to your office leave in disbelief. You urge them to buy an amp, forget their PR postgraduate course and pull off their shellac nails. You tell them it is right to have callouses on the tips of their fingers, that PVC trousers could help them think about their gender conditioning. You urge them to leave the trail of making on their life. To go to scrapyards and haul home car parts, use metal as a way of beating the percussive heart out of the system. It is another language you speak; one lost some time ago on the sticky floors of spent ballrooms. It is you shouting against time. Wishing you still could slip into all those hurriedly made dresses, strap on your army boots and wander down the corridors of power, whistling.

26. British Bulldog

Not having a car who needed a car? In the last dying days of '92 my friend tells tales of travelling from London to get to Yorkshire. He was living in a squat with a Vivienne Westwood model. She did not mind straddling glass tables for golden showers with businessmen. My friend, ex-army, found passion in late-night conversation. Once used to his garrulous ways, we talked late into night, but he was not allowed to hit on me.

A friendship that took years to develop, initially I ran from his authoritative voice. Thrown together as students bewildered in California. Ever on the make, finding ways of not paying for coffee, books and events— how dare he steal a book at the launch of Thom Gunn's *The Man With Night Sweats*? A military past, anarchist mind and devotion to poetry. Witnessing the big argument between my flatmate and her boyfriend he shrugged. "Americans" he stated emphatically "are always so dramatic." One night cradling wine in his glass he told me of hitching up the M1. David Gedge in the background playing his guitar so hard it made his hands bleed, oh the heartbreak of *The Wedding Present*. The driver, a monosyllabic man looked like a boar. Midway, the man asked him to reach for a box on the back seat, in it were six bulldog clips. Following each junction, the driver asked him to attach a clip to a different part of each ear. "What did you do" I asked incredulous, was he spinning a tall tale to ballast his past? "He didn't wince, that was the scary part, I scarpered when we hit the service station." These my friend recalled, were the last dying days of hitchhiking.

27. Scale

"All the new thinking is about loss" wrote the poet who introduced her to American poetry. Entering debates on deconstruction, presence as an illusion, meaning always deferred. But the present is Janus-faced finding appreciation in recollection. Loss offers a linkage to a community of ghosts, a legion of voices. The synapse of earlier perception surely leaves a residue in cognition?

Unwritten in the collective memory of social media, she remains reticent, unwilling to make the past a public forum. The school photo retains its clarity, others are puzzled over familiar names. Is it a burden to feel the asphalt of a warm summer's day and the roll call? Communal recollection overrides personal history. Some continued their education; others fell away after formal exams. The woman who posted the photo tells how she was kicked out from school, pregnant. Faces become fleshier, they blur with age around the cheeks, eyes, neck. Fearful of the loss of love, health.

Attending to loss, she is wire brushing a metal weight used in her grandmother's shop. She handled the weight many times, one of many objects in a shed she felt were keening, needing new purpose. An old metal file removes orange indentations. Washed and dried it requires painting, the flat black protecting the iron. Holding that weight, she held the balance of a former load. The final tilt of the scale, a small sack of potatoes that a farmer picked up every Friday, walking, not having car nor tractor. Baler twine belting his trousers, he would only grunt and cough, there were rumours his cows were starving.

28. Saboteur

If this was a year of magical thinking what do other years become? A year that the library attendant followed you around the stacks with your mother's midwifery bag. You had taken off its navy cover, decanted the instruments: a brittle rubber tube, an enamel tun dish, the stainless steel boxes. You soaked its spotted cotton inlay in tepid water with a splash of bleach, it had loops for sharp metal instruments. The bag, was now a steel box cold to the touch in this Scottish winter. You could be carrying uranium rather than books on media and communication.

The attendant told you that the midwifery bag was banned. Its case made stealing books possible. There were other laws that you broke that year. Saturday morning wearing your boots and the warmest clothes, a flask, a box of sandwiches, piling into the back of a van. "Step On" and "Elephant Stone" on the stereo, sitting on the hard floor. Moving through from motorway to country, hedges high. Into the break of red winter light, the sun's eye. Barks and yelps getting close, the hounds are hungry. This is where you first heard of terrier men. Before the Criminal Justice and Public Order Act 1994, which became known as the "rave" act. 63.1 applied to "gathering in land in the open air of 100 or more persons (whether or not trespassers) at which amplified music was played during the night." This day of travel was before 68.1 a, b and c which enabled prosecution for "aggravated trespass on land in the open air" if you did anything which intended to deter or obstruct any "lawful activity which persons are engaging in." Shouted, jeered, mocked, spat at. Horses high above men with florid cheeks, hooves made repetitive circles on the yard. You feel the *anti-mate* spray in the pocket of your big army surplus coat, ready for the run.

29. Memoir Motif

In autobiography there is the sense of height, of seeing from a great distance. Not over a maze, hills, or valleys but over something that although unknowable becomes *known*. There are moments of growth.

For example, the child from the village goes to the city. The child from the village then-living-in-the-city, returns to the village filled with an understanding of something other. In the village nobody except a grandmother, reads this understanding and warns the child. For others the understanding is arrogance, a failing, a refusal to act as they might need the child to act. The villagers want to be proud of the child that went to the city and returned. But the child is not the same. They ignore the difference. The child puts them on edge, an animal returning with a new smell. Defamiliarised. The adult self writes a book about what understanding might mean, attempts to "tell their story". In truth, this is not as it happened. Leaving the country of her language the child feels a failing from afar. As the language empties from the village, changes cannot be contained. Post offices close, shopkeepers retire, local schools becomes community centres. Place names change, the history of origins is unreliable. The slow stories which fuelled fire-lit-nights are tangled with political dissent. Needing form before their reanimation.

30. Protest

Acting politically in public enthrals you. Do you remember those early protests, going to demonstrations in unfamiliar cities? The time you took your friends from Scotland to a Welsh language demonstration in Cardiff. Never part of a coterie of Welsh speakers, time away from your language, the scorn of Scottish voices: *Wales is a what ... a Principality?* Made you want to connect. The day you saw a boy from your comprehensive, he gave love bites at discos. Now with a red aerosol at the Welsh Office, well before devolution, grey suited men held court with quangos. You watched, thinking "he snogged me once." Everyone came to the back of the bus, watching you both.

Now you were watching him, knowing he's preparing to get caught, an act of civil disobedience in the name of language. Slowly and with great attention, he sprays the words *Deddf Eiddo* on the white pillar, demanding affordable housing in Welsh communities. The paint drips like blood, next to the dragon's tongue, the symbol for *Cymdeithas*. The police see it too, a communal action, cued perfectly, staged for a dramatic exit. You salute your school crush, whose political opinions had been muted in school; he will be held in a cell, a first act followed by others.

Your university is known throughout Scotland for having staged a demonstration at the Queen's visit, she was hit with an egg. For years, images of the Queen appeared with a blast of yolk, a speech bubble "we are not amused". Another state visit, Thatcher passed through Scotland on her Poll Tax tour. A slim student of psychology with a steady boyfriend, threw a can at the car slowly climbing the cobble road up to the castle. It bounced into an ancient gutter, with a shrug, the police took her into custody. That was the closest you ever got to meeting a Prime Minister.

31. Unigate Foods Ltd or, Notes to a dying mother in law

Notes written on spare churn tags my grandmother left in a drawer. She used these tags for grocery lists delivered by the village store once a week. Recycled for calculating accounts, money owed and given. I was too young to remember the churns ever being collected, platforms on farm lanes a reminder. We would perform dramas, gesturing at the small boxlike cars of the 70s. Script on brown cardboard gives the story of farming in an earlier time. "Warranted Pure New Milk: Sweet, clean without preservatives. Sold by Milk Marketing Board under their prescribed contract. Unigate Foods Limited under the Board's Sale Contract (SEE OVER)" I turn over to find an account of her dying mother in law. Notes alternating between Welsh and English "Supper was given at quarter to eight filled the hot water bottle at 2.15 am." My great grandmother preferred a stone bottle wrapped in a small woollen blanket. "Did not pass water until 3.30am then at 7:30 am, I slept in parlour with her all night 20th February. She went back to bed a 4.15pm until 6pm with supper from 7-7.30pm, bed again at 8.50pm a hot water bottle at 10pm, then 11pm then 12am. On the 23rd February the doctor came. She rang the bell at 2:25am kept her in the chair until 3 am. Rang the bell 4am did not answer it, got up at 5am to get some tablets and took a look at her, she was awake. She ate at 8am" this is where the account ends. You recall a slight woman with a bun and crocheted hat showing you that snakes meant loss and ladders gain. She hated cut flowers, wore and washed her cotton aprons until they were soft with age. And stared at you with the bluest eyes.

32. Curating a space for anachronistic design

We are mindful of that space where objects retain their usefulness, not yet dated. But no longer telling the current story of our consumption. Until one summer they might be discovered again. Bakelite transmissions PARIS/ BREMEN/ LUXEMBOURG/ DLF/ WDR, the mono cassette player offering better noise that your laptop. A found boxed card, in lurid psychedelic colours celebrating your birth, a letter slips out. In translation:

"Congratulations on your precious gift of a daughter. I am so delighted that you are getting better and healing, I hope that you return home soon. We will come and see you soon, we ask after you frequently. Your mother tells me she is very happy the birth went well. We miss seeing you at the chapel on Sunday and our incidental chats. We had the rehearsal for the *Gymanfa Ganu* here yesterday and the numbers were low considering three chapels were meeting, however there was considerable amount of eating in the vestry. The weather is still rather mixed, we've just started our cut of hay, but it remains to be collected. You are very lucky to have the summer as your season of motherhood, you'll be able to show your girl the world. I will sign off now and hope that we will have a good chat soon. P.S. and kisses to the baby" (your name misspelt).

Cards that are kept, establish an archive, alerting us to something larger than ourselves. One birth impacts a community, a language. Why cry over the viscose, threads of writing which represent an overflow of feeling? Puffy-eyed you think of those words "a most precious daughter" given by one having none.

33. A Crystal Bell

There was a time before these C roads were flickering images, that you walked them. Positing the yellow human at the top of each farm entrance, high hedges with recycling bins, to make a sense of space. Places unimaginable only visited once the owner was ill, dying or dead. At least this is how you saw it when your mother a district nurse was asked to visit, rather than "bother" the surgery doctors. You went along, it could be changing a dressing, monitoring blood pressure or laying out a body. Things she did, a small community, the people shy and scared of medicine. Or, some were just insistent, they shopped at your grandmother's village shop, nursing care became optional extra. "Why do they think I like looking at their sores, wounds and hurt bodies" your mother asked aloud.

Once upon a time, two cousins had married, they had no children only a labourer by the name of Meic who lived in a loft over the stable. Meic adored his employers but never married, never owned anything. You remember visiting the farm at the age of ten, the old lady in her 90s showed you a crystal bowl that sounded like a bell. "Listen" she said flicking her nail against its side, they ate with broken cutlery, you watched her chasing an egg on her plate with a two-pronged fork. Her brother trained as a doctor and died young. In time, both she and her husband died, Meic found his first home. An old age bungalow with hot water and central heating. On sunny days you would see Meic sitting on his doorstep, with a group chatting. You wondered how he adapted to leisure, released from service at the age of eighty. You had watched his face in awe of the crystal, the lit fire, framing the kitchen, the steep staircase your mother climbed, the husband, ill in bed. Meic carrying the contents of a commode, having spent his life tending the animals, now caring for his employers.

You did not want to go out in that dark night: your mother said, "come with me, this is life you will never see again."

34. Exhibit A

After the owners of the farm died, the family held an auction, there were no children. Your mother said the family found so many boxes in the attic, a brother's medical archive, *the doctor who died young.* They contacted her about medical textbooks published in the 1890s. These included *Diseases of The Skin* and *Nervous Diseases.* They did not know what to do with a collection of books with plates of disturbed patients, contorted, illustrations of lesions on bodies.

Later they told her about the skeleton they had found. The skeleton had scared them in the attic, real bone accompanied with a polished wooden pole for hanging. The skeleton came from India in the 1890s, they were scared of *this thing,* decided it must be removed. Worse, they decided it had to be destroyed. A group of men had smashed the skeleton. They buried it in one of the fields. The child thought what if the skeleton was found and a murder investigation began, like *Cadno Farm* in Pendine? The child learns of the medical trade in bodies and skeletons, how skeletons were shipped from India for classroom demonstrations. The mother greets it as a calamity; she could have given it to a friend who teaches biology: he has only a plastic skeleton. Once he had given her a revision lesson and the mother thought her school had "not gone deep enough into it."

The child pictured him excavating the site, methodically placing the bones in order on a sackcloth: *the leg bone's connected to the knee bone, the knee bone's connected to the thigh bone, the thigh bone's connected to the hip bone.* Watching *The Singing Detective,* she was half in love with the main character, thinking through his latest dime novel on a ward bandaged and broken. Years later she thought of the family's violence, how her mother's solution was equally gothic. What would the students have made of the clean teeth and small frame? Some years after, she visits the farm and wonders what that act inscribed, having a different vocabulary she understands the word *postcolonial,* but that is a different story.

35. Inhabiting

A square house in the middle of the country. Easily broken into, set alight, your flagstones quarried and fire tiles taken (with cast iron surround). Recently emptied, scalped for a sale after a long let (two sisters and one brother now deceased). Tenant farmers, a smallholding, a brook and trees full of crow chorus. You knew all three, found the alcoholic brother's empty whiskey bottles thrown into the river, when wading to tickle trout. A silky feeling of fear in your hands. Two sisters also unmarried, one spoke broken Welsh, the other stroked your hair, having nothing to say. You would be sent there to deliver a bill from your grandmother, or a loaf of bread.

In the overcrowded sitting room, there were chalk figures of women, arms outstretched, dogs sitting in baskets one ear cocked. Jugs advertising *Teachers*, *Bells*, *Black & White Scotch*. The brother a bad drunk and rudimentary farmer kept fear in the house, quieter once weaned off the hard stuff. A doctor told him to drink the small bottles of pop your grandmother sold. You find the house bare, only a ghetto blaster, candlelit.

The owner's daughter hosts a party before the house is sold. First year of college you have all returned, migratory. What to wear for these people, Oxblood Dr. Martens, a 1970s paisley print dress, shiny aquamarine leggings like the ones Bjork wore singing Icelandic with The Sugar Cubes? The sound of drum 'n' bass, laughter, shouts mixing Welsh with English. Friends of the past stubbing out their cigarettes on lintels, loving one another in corners, on stairways, near the cowshed. Brushing past them to bedrooms, the cartography of rooms previously unseen. You imagined thin curtains, a heavy armoire against the wall, and nailed a *Though Shalt Not* above the bed.

36. Ty Haf †

This story starts the year the Cocteau Twins release *Heaven or Las Vegas*. You saw Grangemouth's colours, the chemical plant was an inspiration for the 4AD record cover. Though you never shared this information with anyone until now. The year you get to know the owner of the second home near your village.

She is researching a PhD, has made friends with your grandmother, walking down to the shop between periods of writing. Your grandmother tells her about your A-Level results, how you are studying English and Film far away. The woman is surprised that you go to university. She is not patronising, she was a housewife, a mother of three, the good wife of a somebody who works in a global auction house. As a smoker the daily journey to your grandmother's shop becomes a ritual.

Home one summer, about to study in California. Before the interview, you swore you will not use the word "invigorate" and promptly did. An afternoon party at the second home. Walking close to hedgerows, to the farmhouse. Home to a doctor's skeleton that is now buried in the field. While you are hungry for discussions of Akhmatova, you are a spectacle in a cabaret of curiosities. These people mean well with their cheese, biscuits, wine and olives. But it seems derisory that the milking parlour is now a games room. They are polite, tell you about Californian sights you have yet to see. Something however screams inside, throwing imaginary typewriters against the newly pointed stone walls. You want to cut the green baize of the snooker table with a sturdy kitchen knife.

---

†   Translates as "summer house". It is reported that almost 40% of properties sold in Gwynedd (N. Wales) between March 2019 and April 2020 were purchased as second homes (See note 1.) In 2022 it was reported that 7.3% houses were sold as second homes compared with 1.7% across the UK. (See note 2.)

37. Auxiliary

The summer that she fell out spectacularly with her mother, she learned the importance of the brakes on hospital beds. Working as an auxiliary on an orthopaedic ward taught her that. The ward moved from the first floor to the basement, immobile patients with hip replacements. Ball and socket– the demand of moving patients painlessly into lifts, down corridors, into the new ward named Ceri, short for Ceridwen or perhaps love. Forever, she will recall the wife bleached white by anaesthesia, shaping her lips in magenta before visiting hour. Her squat husband came to her bedside each night to hold her hand.

A summer that tested a relationship based on a shared obsession with music, which failed. Not from a lack of passion but care, the games he played, a relationship that paused early in its imagining. The most humiliating date. She arranged to meet after her shift in a pub. Changing clothes at a friend's house. The day of her first death on the ward. Swift and immediate: a cardiac arrest, the crash team could do nothing. Outside on the corridor, she saw the paddles applied, shock administered. Recounting what she saw to her friend, offered only disconnection, the patient was new, name unknown.

She was late and changed from the bottle green uniform into a floral vintage dress. Black tights and blue suede Mary Janes, a green rayon cardigan. At the pub in town she was sober, he with his mates, intent on ignoring her. Tired of hanging round, bored of drunken male conversation she decides to go, he tells her "loosen up". Unblinking she stares, she'd loved his tawny skin, his brown eyes, his shyness – it takes ten years to tell him what happened that night (and day).

38. Smallholding

You have spent an important part of life thinking in baths. There are the winter baths – the enamel never warms, steam billowing, willing the downstairs fire lit. The summer bath – a window, people entering the village, speaking in low voices, moving their animals. I am not referencing here Bonnard's bath where a woman appears meditating on her being, an open window.

This is the slow summer, small farms still exist, no need for contractors, mixed farms produced many things. No need to worry about the old bridge buckling under megatractors. Now a hundred acres is not enough, the pursuit of productivity increases the need for fertilizers. "First crop, second crop, third crop the grass is blue" your father shakes his head. As his father shook his head, a great reader of *The Reader's Digest.* You read 'Laugher is the Best Medicine", marvelling at their monthly giveaways: plastic and gold keys promising to unlock new houses and cars. Grandfather teaching the chain of effect: fertilizer spread on soil travels to water, a system of feeding and breeding. "NITRATES" he'd spit; making potions from dandelion and burdock, celery seeds for rheumatism, marshmallow and slippery elm on cuts and bruises. Before going green became another form of consumption.

"Look" your father says, at the flock, of seagulls descending on the village ten miles inland. Sea birds feeding, manure generated by indoor cows, the farm of the future, a thousand acres. So much muck earthworms cannot breathe coming up for air; the gulls know fast food. In time the earthworm population decreases. Soil loses its small tunnels, capillaries of air. Balding land appears framed by dock leaves and nettles. The price of emptied land.

39. New Romantics

A thrill a day keeps the chill away, love like a dagger and a sound like a wymowhey. Fame on your wall, wearing lip gloss and tight leather trousers, is made possible by access to art school. There are days when home feels like a ghost town but it's OK since you still have pride. A warrior well into post-punk at the age of ten. *You may not like the things we say. What's the difference anyway?*

Always SKA in the air, everybody in your primary school class is obsessed with two tone. Influenced by brothers and sisters in the big glass comprehensive named after the 19th century educator, Gruffydd Jones. You get brave, are smuggled into discos – teenagers smoking, cans passed round the back of the hall. Days of trainers, a t-shirt and jeans, if you are lucky a donkey jacket or parka. Your dad wears a donkey jacket to the factory, once you tried it on. The jacket in the airing cupboard, its back marked *MMB: Milk Marketing Board* smelling of rancid butter and cigarettes. Dad a shift worker, a semi-skilled fitter supervising packing. He returns with cuts on his hands, metal slivers under skin. Trying to fix fragile jets one morning, the machine restarted, spraying hot glue onto his face, the scar gradually became smaller. A thread of copper flew into his eye, the iris became emerald green. You administered the drops those days when your mother was not home.

One evening, you decided to "fix" his hands. Warm water, bubble bath, you soaked them cleaning stubborn oil from under his nails with a manicure set given at Christmas. Even at ten you knew he was happy when you applied moisturiser on his scars.

40. Score for the Voice

Getting a musical education is not hard where you live. Although your references are electric. You cannot read music but read *sol-fa*. You know your Bach but not your Rachmaninov. The local postmaster is called Handel, which makes your best friend, a seventy-year-old jazz pianist, crease his eyes with laughter.

You have been trained by your Sunday school and father to enunciate lyrics, to place inflection on words. This colouring of the text is emphasised in a small book inherited from your grandmother *The Reciter's School*. In Welsh, it shows you the declamatory nature of recitation, each picture with arms and legs in various poses. How to maintain the rhythm of breath. You are alert to the relationship between body and text, the poem offers musicality. So, when you read "Projective Verse" at twenty, its focus on breath and writing, breath as a unit of measure, or a unit of thought comes as no surprise.

Performance and the musicality of words were always inseparable. Memorising poems, performing them on stage reading the judges' comments. "She was going well until she stumbled over the word *vainglorious*", "she shook her head too much", "at times I felt this child misunderstood the poem". You became familiar with critics' tongues. Adults stating, "you were swindled". At seven, adults reiterated your felt injustice. At nine you rebelled, no longer wanting a competitive stage for poems. What you wanted was a microphone. The poem is a score for the voice, you were looking for a jukebox and a bass guitar.

41. Getting a Musical Education

Time passes, an intense desire to be elsewhere, beyond the constraints of the linguistic community you love, everyone seeking departure. An unhappiness so deep, it cannot be lanced by the vicarious actions of friends, who get drunk, embrace strangers while wearing black leather gloves. Only one decent nightclub in the town. You harangue the DJ for music: The Cure, New Order, Echo and the Bunnymen. The economic necessity of pleasing an audience seeking the music of daytime radio, Stock Aitken Waterman the cover versions, one night, you've had enough.

Two people move into the village; she owns the house: he is her partner. This bedraggled angel saves you (at the time you thought you were saving him). He offers you a musical education. They make teenage life tolerable, anarchic and idiosyncratic. He taught his partner to play the piano, dyslexic she began by reading notes in a different order. They painted crochets and quavers on kitchen tiles, a lesson in everydayness. He swooned at her playing Schubert, declared she revived his love of classical music after a lifetime of jazz. Each visit he brought new duets to play. When they fought he took his satchel filled with compositions. They loved you equally for the difference they brought to your life. Brief enthusiasms were infectious. A night spent tie-dyeing every t-shirt, bound in string, buckets of pink, purple and red.

No longer going to nightclubs you listened to hyperbolic stories, sat in an inglenook, cradling a lurcher's head. You walk up the hill to their cottage to hear strains of music. Wait with me, outside the window while they play the baby grand, marvel at their slight sway, in tune with one another.

42. Welsh Independence

The couple in the longhouse introduce her to Bossa Nova. The spines of their LPs bear the scratch marks of cats. She learns how Sinatra is a master of enunciation; the racism faced by Sammy Davis Jnr. How Count Basie really did have a monogrammed dressing gown. She takes to playing the cassettes recorded during long conversations. Driving C roads she plays Getz and Gilberto, sometimes Bessie Smith.

In the sixth form common room she scorns daytime radio. *Our Song*: love's desperate circumstances. She sabotages its manipulation, with The Pistols, "Mississippi Goddam" and "Cristion yn y Kibbutz". Collecting music becomes a religion. No vinyl except for a small market stall that sells her a Velvet Underground LP: it is only when she listens to "The Gift" that she realises John Cale is from Ammanford.

The couple in the longhouse introduced her to Beethoven's late string quartets, one rule: never talk, classical music is not wallpaper. As a hotel piano player he listened to hours of chat. He loathes The Beatles, which marked the end of live jazz; pop meant DJs and dances, gone was his trio. Pop left him playing improvisations in bars, waiting for cues in overheard conversations, recalibrating "Send in the Clowns". If he could spot a romance, or hear a birthday mentioned it could mean a tip. This was when he began to drink from boredom, the chatter of hotel lobbies. Gin at the end of the keyboard, his right hand could meet the glass with the flourish of a chord. One Christmas he said "Look, they know their customer" holding out a bright green Christmas card. "I'd worry" his partner snorted "when a distillery starts sending you greeting cards."

43. 1991

Why bother reading a fragments of the lives of others in this rule-governed way? I thought if I took twenty lines for each chapter I could write in the midst of emailing, screen notifications, actions that are not *me* but have become something of *what I am*. Is the alternative to become the curator of texts, to sculpt with words?

My answer might be this story of waking up on the floor of the night before. The home of final year students who are now your friends. Your best friend is seeing the editor of the university magazine. You are both second years, impertinent in your charity shop dresses with matching psychedelic headbands for an event called *Petal Politique*. You still have the badge of that night somewhere, the editor DJed to a group of the coolest people you'd seen. Early '90s men and women wearing American workmen's dungarees, 1940s suits and hats, women's wedge cuts, striped tights, pierced noses and 1960s leather jackets, everybody smoking. Bowie's *Low* at the chill out party, nervous amidst the incestuous signalling. Your friend had told you of love triangles, being introduced to scowling girls who were ex-lovers.

Beside you is the first boy you fell for in your first week, floppy-haired, dressed in a grandfather shirt, vintage slacks and a oversized pullover. He appeared at gigs and would then disappear. A graduate living in the city coming on campus to see friends. Shy, he competes for your attention with a philosopher who engages you, but over explains. Decades before *mansplaining* entered your lexicon, you nod, small glances at the floppy haired boy next to you. Birds sing, everyone too stoned to talk, you crawl into the thin sleeping bag. When you wake you leave the chalet as silently as your army boots allow, someone snores gently. That evening your friend returns your green scrunchie, the boy-man wore it on his wrist all day, she'd asked for its return. "Vanishing Point" plays in the background.

44. Isn't Anything

The immensity of recollection cradled in the briefest song. "Instrumental No 2" by my bloody valentine places you 30 years ago, a ghetto blaster, gas fire, a damp cottage in Dunblane. Several years before the tragedy of small children is forever associated with the town. The need for warmth, hot water, the battle for washing. Clothes smell of mildew spores and smoke. Rooms small and overstuffed with furniture. Trails on the carpet, you have been teaching yourself to roller skate with white boots from a charity shop. Wednesday evening bell ringing practice at the cathedral over the road. Their long pauses or minimalism becomes irritating, you write with earplugs.

The first friend you made in fresher's week copied the rare 7 inch by my bloody valentine. The song marries a moment between dance and lyricism, though there are no words. While days are dark and time between writing long, you cook listening to their *Tremolo* EP: "Honey Power" and "Moon Song". This annoys your housemate who is grappling with the philosophy of time and a man named John McTaggart. Little did you know that the rare 7 inch, a free single with the first 5,000 LP copies of the band's album *Isn't Anything* eventually becomes downloadable. Your library of music carried in rucksacks, an old record player whose speakers sometimes falter into fuzz.

Another housemate trains to make limestone render for 17th century walls. She supplements her income with a papier-mâché vase factory in the front room. Blowing up weather balloons, paste and newspaper the creations take shape, set, are painted, tattooed with images, water coloured and glazed. Out of economy you shop in charity shops, the pursuit of the good jumper, or a 70s coat that will keep you warm this winter. That valentine's day, your boyfriend's gift: a toy painted guitar as a card, in that once sleeping town, before it was named by the world.

45. Frontier West

A summer of dancing barefoot round a mono cassette player. Moments of understanding what a body can do. Trailing her mother on district visits in the seaside towns of West Wales. The passenger of school holidays, hoping for a comic and a tin of pop. A Chrysler Sunbeam, acid green, stereo, hatchback and racing stripes. Near the sea you'd listen endlessly to Adam and the Ants' *Kings of the Wild Frontier*.

Monitoring babies, cleaning and bandaging bed sores, vitamin B12 injections given to alcoholics, removing stitches of those returned from surgery, slighter, quieter yet still smoking. The daughter was obsessed with working class men wearing lip gloss, billowing in cotton shirts, part Errol Flynn, part council estate, cartoonish vignettes on Saturday screens. She saw Adam's album in the mobile home of a pregnant girl, FRONTIER: its implications of genocide and the continuation of settler histories.

First-time mothers seemed so far from you, taking responsibility, making a home against circumstances of perilous employment. Later Adam in the tabloids, the world sniggering at his fall into the arms of law. Bloated and balding, he suffered episodes of mania and the leaden weight of depression. In her thirties, she later reads that the singer is mangled by his own mental health, hospitalised to a secure unit. She finds the address on a message board and sends a card. He gave her a vocabulary for understanding post-punk-populism, an asexual dream world, where she became a buccaneer, a pirate for minority languages.

The card sent was *Alice in Wonderland*'s croquet, the flamingos as mallets. She told him how his lyrics created a language of rebellion in a town where the school disco was the highlight of the year. She wished him good health, sleep and peace. Months later in an envelope marked "insufficient postage" a drawing of her reading, hair in a ponytail under the arc of an Anglepoise. *Love and Thanks Adam Ant.*

46. Say Hello, Wave Goodbye

At night, a mother and daughter come to the front door of a bungalow in a small town. They come once every week, I do my homework on the new breakfast bar. They use my bedroom.

The daughter used to make fun of me ridiculing my trainers and page boy hairstyle during walks to buy cigarettes for my father. He sent me down the road, during long summer holidays. Being too tired after a night shift, he would give extra money to buy whatever I wanted. Explosive moon dust, liquorice strings, a bag of gold rush chewing gum in an imitation cloth bag. Each time the shopkeeper asked disapprovingly: "These are not for you are they?" Girls in the secondary modern smoked. The daughter had that tainted-love-soft cell-eyeliner and a fringe that swept to the left. As tough as the studded bracelets and belts that she wore.

One evening my mother wanted to broach "something". Had she noticed the name of my current crush on a notebook with a small curlicue for a heart? "Your bedroom, is being used for a young girl so that I can check she's OK, she is pregnant. She is going to have the baby soon." "Is she scared?" was the only thing I could think to ask. The doppler, checking blood pressure, in a room with volumes of Edith Nesbit, posters of Duran Duran and a framed picture of an embroidered hare. I imagined my mother doing all the things I'd seen before: petroleum jelly on a swollen belly, easing the doppler out of its velour lined case, placing it on skin, the sudden swoosh into the speaker. *Thud thud Thud – Thud thud Thud* smiles, the slight gasps. When she heard her baby, did she turn towards my Holly Hobbie washbag or did she look up at Simon Le Bon's tanned face, his streaked hair?

47. Adulting

The child meets her mother in the car park, it is spring, she carries a graffitied satchel. In the car, sits the teenager that once had medical examinations in her bedroom. The child knows not to mention this. The teenager smiles, she is wearing her school uniform too. Her mother asks "how did your French test go?" – the child answers that it was OK mentions that she'd like to attend the youth camp in North Wales and learn to canoe.

The journey home is not far, the radio introduces "Together in Electric Dreams". The soundtrack of a summer, a video with bursts of light, a pulsing network connecting lover and beloved. Her town is changing, its centre is now devolved. Concrete alcoves and walkways, three decades from now this shopping centre will decentre once more, shops will be built in the spaces where animals once cried and were sold. A bartering of lives marked by a drover with sheep in bronze opposite the multiplex cinema. Children sit on the sheep and pretend to race, but they are locked, eating or thinking about the future. All this is yet to happen.

The child, now a middle-aged woman, questions her mother that afternoon how it feels to swell into pregnancy too young? "We'd been with the registrar to sign the death certificate of her baby" she answers, "her parents refused. The registrar didn't look up when he asked her who the father was, the baby's name. She looked at me, a complete blank, I suggested a band maybe she liked, she said Simon and that was it." The daughter thought of the tiny sculpted graves she had seen in country graveyards. Her mother continued: "The family didn't want a funeral, an undertaker buried the baby as part of another burial." The daughter remembered hearing a teacher speaking decades ago and her stomach curdled. "Poor girl, everyone saw how her body ballooned, she was once such a pretty thing."

48. People's Park

A friend wanted to know what it was to be a woman. He did not identify as female but wanted to get as close to the experience of being *seen* as a young woman. Early '90s at Ashby Flea market we talked about this while inspecting a 60s floral clasp handbag, he told me "go get that". "Do you really think so?" I asked knowing it would have little practical use travelling across the US.

Even then, it was difficult being a female pedestrian, I frequently stumbled into areas that instantly felt unsafe, unknown mappings. Not wanting to offend, I bought the bag for $5, it held things of value safe but never walked with me in army surplus boots. My friend read *The Martyrs: Joan of Arc to Yitzhak Rabin* in the dorm canteen while he ate his salad and ramen. His plan was daring and dangerous. He would test what it might mean to be *seen* at a fraternity party. It took weeks of planning. Stockings, kitten heels, a full face of make-up and delicate items of jewellery with a body tube dress. He shaved his legs, another friend trained his curls to fall to one side, his lips a blush pink. He had studied movement, and went with a sorority member who loathed her house.

When we next met, he smiled sadly; it had been easy, most of the party were drunk already. But the intensity of their gaze had thrown him "nothing prepared me for male hunger." Near a beer keg, a frat boy stroked his bottom, time he thought, to leave. "How do women deal with this" he asked gently "that hunger, fear, men's need to be acknowledged?" Later that year my friend slept out in the historic park associated with campus unrest and homelessness. He heard the muffled cries and frequent screams of those lying under bushes, near chain-link fences. It was terrifying – he didn't dare look.

49. Hungry Ghost

Years of a belligerent shyness, assuming not to be an object of anyone's desire. Elements of performance, perennial observation. A low risk enterprise, people watching. You focussed on the actions of confident women but now think about them in different terms.

Crossing the border for Christmas, five taking a bus to meet another five in Baja California. The language for this form of experience: tourism, economic opportunism. Friends chattering with the confidence of blue jays. Listening to the music of 1991 Lush's *Gala*, Ride's *Going Blank Again*, the bus moved down the peninsula, to the last watchful stop. Factions in the group, the friction of unspent sexual attraction, you became a group of three hitch hiking to Loreto. A final lift in an empty fish van, boot lined with ice.

You, smiled and explained your way into town. The need to find a supermarket, your period had started, you wondered if they sold tampons in a Catholic town. A young man stared briefly at you, discreetly you hid your purchase walking into sun to meet the other two, thirsty and leaden with cramping. What to do next, there was no guidebook, you were hungry, confused by the rift in the group. "Where are you from" - it was the young man, his name was Ariel, a marine biologist. "Stay at mine tonight, while you wait for your friends to come tomorrow." Only one small hotel in town, Ariel knew the rest would end up there. A puppy, Tico, greeted them in an unfinished home, concrete blocks, no windows. You kept thinking of your thin light sleeping bag while sitting round a fire with wine and bread. You accepted his invitation to sleep under stars in the dusty garden, talking softly until sleep came.

50. Mission

Reunited, we told them about the puppy, the sea, the family with young children nearby. And Ariel the marine biologist with shark teeth nailed into a wall. A song on rewind replay *Before I met you I was blind.* Nothing that morning was natural or neutral, an edge of performance in the reunited group. You were new once more, but what would your best friend make of the concrete hut? They told us of a falling out with another couple, (part of the grand reunion), in this sharing we hugged once more. You told your friend how the constellations gave you vertigo: "Sleeping under the stars?" she quizzed smiling.

Christmas was close, being from a cold climate we spent the day watching pelicans dive. A party at Ariel's listening to Dylan: *Everybody must get stoned.* Your friend asks about the trophies on the wall. "I will never give them away; each one was a difficult situation." My friend's head cocked; cigarette held in *that* gesture. Christmas Eve we went in Ariel's pickup to the abandoned Misión San Francisco Javier de Viggé–Biaundó.

You imagined the Jesuits creating the church, a compound next to a spring, attempting to make the Cochimi disciples of Christ. The Cochimi tempted by their cooked food, giving up their nomadism. Finally decimated by European gifts of smallpox and measles. You paced along flagstones; the church preserved, a stray dog licked your hand. Later that night, after midnight mass, we sang cradling the dark, already older. Somebody placed a lollipop on each pillow asking us to be children. My friend, her bed unslept did not sneak into morning, but made her entrance. A shark tooth shining from the leather lace around her neck.

51. Lyrical Invention

Coming from this "little shit place", as a rugby coach told us in 2018, we learn adaptive strategies. We are mountain people, under the radar, speaking a language that offers protection from direct penetration. Home is broken down, parables of post-industrial, an adventure campground for another country.

Of course, relish the description by A.A. Gill we are "loquacious, dissemblers, immoral liars, stunted, bigoted, dark, ugly, pugnacious little trolls." Or, maybe dear reader, if you are into the burn Jeremy Clarkson appeals: "It's entirely unfair that some people are born fat or ugly or dyslexic or disabled or ginger or small or Welsh. Life, I'm afraid, is tragic." My friends this tragic life, as we sit in our demesne in soft rainfall. Ron Liddle's "miserable, seaweed munching, sheep-bothering pinch-faced hill-tribes" comes into mind. Journalists who want our words silenced as "an appalling and moribund monkey language." There is a danger in responding too quickly, giving ugly words a permanence, credibility.

Monolingualism is no crime, the curation of other languages is a tricky art, but monoculturalism, the impossibility of fielding doubt into your rhetoric? Doubt makes me wonder if there is a salt mill grinding in the sea. Or, that those mountains are fashioned by a giant god, breathing into life birds, trees and stones. Being didactic creates its own loss, disabling, poor creature with open mouth signing into the world. Leviathans straddling the shapes of their own grammar, splish-splosh. Instead, recall how Benjamin Britten's *This Little Babe* translates into your language. Echolalia, how to find narrative accuracy not in the repetition of words, but in timing to music. Caught on quarter inch tape, a reel packaged and sent. "Oh, yes the choral" you nod "that old stereotype". No, what I reference is the force of *me, you, us* a power of breath to fall and rise without issuing demands. Being here, colouring a lyric's final iteration high notes fading against a cupola, the roof of a tin shed, the gambrel of a village hall, all the mercury bubbles unleashed.

52. Not Daguerreotype

The child finds a picture of a man in a chrome picture frame with a large hanging chain. The picture had been placed in the bottom drawer of a chest with a collection of quilted birthday cards. Housed in small flat boxes, pink bows and silver keys feature on many. Also a round pocket mirror, a picture in lurid orange on the back: "Mont St Michel" written underneath. A small gold torpedo shell, reveals a stub of orange lipstick.

The man's steady gaze upon her, colourised bright blue, unlike any photograph the child has seen before. The cheeks rouged, lips stained crimson, hair a block of auburn. She has grown up with men wearing eyeliner, blusher and eye shadow on TV. Songs of love with anger and melancholy. This man does not seem to be intentionally wearing makeup. A white carnation on his jacket. The background is fuzzy, the man's eyes stare, his face becomes unfriendly. His eyes strain beyond the camera, focusing on a beam of light, trying not to ruin the pose.

The photograph unlike photographs returned by FREEPOST. The spots of time they chronicle already forgotten, as they tumble through a letterbox. Pink ovals over heads, light beams into red starburst. Ghost-faced people with bright red eyes grinning manically. The child, though not long in the world, understands that the photograph is not ancient, he wears no hat, his face is not frozen into a scowl. She has seen antique photos of men stuffed into shirts sitting before a painted pastoral, hard hands stretching beyond cuffs, staring into space. To this most formal frame, she whispers "Hello grandfather devil".

53. Happy in Language

While we walk the estuary one dull January day, my friend tells me that in a recent UK poll our accents are considered the unsexiest. The same poll notes that they are also the "happiest sounding".

The country I now live in has the most attractive accent, who cannot resist a "little Irish brogue". On this trip another friend tells me that *Cymdeithas* have lost the campaign to retain a University hall as a Welsh speaking environment. "But it is being reported a victory" I say. He shakes his head, explains the intricacies of funding, renovations have been given to a global consortium, who will sell this capital asset to the highest bidder. "Who knows which corporation will own the building, once the heart of political action, certainly not the institution."

Near the estuary, I reminisce how we were introduced because of our shared language. Laughing because we both feared that initial meeting, done out of politeness to English friends. Normally we did not seek out exilic communities. We wondered at the homogenisation that "accent" in the article implied – she has words for objects, and I have other words. Can the monolingual ear not discern a shift from region, area, north, south, east to west? Possibly it relishes that deafness yet is able to discern the blend of a coffee, a wine's vintage, a sample on a dance track but hears us as all as same, in our *unsexiness*. My mentor could discern the difference between the most intricate of literary theories. But was surprised that trains travelled to my market town. Showing little curiosity about spaces of linguistic difference on that small island, off the European mainland. We chatted eagerly about the group of *linguistically innovative* poets who challenged the status of public language. Never speaking of my own bilingualism as a way of understanding "ideolectical practices." I dream of languages acidic in their enunciation. To create a language whose very difference inspires revolt.

54. The Art of Confession

She learnt quickly that Americans had a way of revealing, considered in her culture as slightly narcissistic, but described here as art. "Literature & Art" included a creative writing assignment. A mature student told her that she was relishing the opportunity. Theirs was a friendship made tangible over coffee and an elaborate story about a hut on Bali Beach, an ex-boyfriend immobilised by opium.

Unsure whether this was intended to shock or whether she was a co-conspirator to confession, she nodded throughout. Wearing a 1970s zipper red jacket and blue trousers from *Savers*, she was inexperienced and very young. They read and studied self-portraits, two works changed her: Ashbery's *Self Portrait in a Convex Mirror* and Hayden Herrera's *Frida*. This being the early nineties, Kahlo was yet to be on a Prime Minister's wrist, while negotiating Britain's exit from the EU. Her favourite paintings were "Frida and Diego" and Rivera's "The Flower Carrier". The latter showed the burden of work, a man on his knees, an enormous basket of flowerheads strapped to his back. A woman attempts to help him, at first glance the flowers could be plums. Later, she becomes alert to the ghost of *Treasure Island* in the bay where Rivera designed a mural *Pan American Unity*; he kept working even after the Fair closed in 1940, and it was boxed in crates.

Other works such as Virginia Woolf's *Moments of Being* felt overwrought, she was tired of epiphanic spots of time. She worried about her uneventful assignment, did it capture her biography? It could in fact be told in a couple of sentences: working hard, achieving mobility. Her friend found it easy, she relished writing about her troubled brother, the mother–daughter dyad, her affairs with lecturers and philosophers. She in turn could only think of her community, the people who wished her well on her year abroad, the gift from a bad-tempered neighbour of a red dragon tea towel. Her grandmother at the centre of the village trading petrol, pink paraffin, stamps in a tin, loose potatoes, a slab of cheddar. The madness her grandmother tended, the community's peculiarities, and petty vendettas – how to inscribe these dynamics in a thousand words? The grades back her friend with an A+ and her own middling B with the bald comment "nice portrait but surely such sentimentality cannot be true?"

55. Box of Breath

Writing on the day of difficulties, a tempo of commemoration in my head. The day you woke early, a Sunday morning, difficulty catching your breath, feeling ill. You who complained little, looked pale and scared but had dressed and made your bed downstairs (the stairs being difficult).

Earlier that year you had called after vomiting what looked like coffee granules. "B made a flask when she took me to the seaside yesterday- her coffee was too strong." The stomach lining aggravated after two aspirin a day. "It gives me a boost, a real lift" you told the doctor ruefully. This January morning, in the stone longhouse, scrabbling for a nebuliser, put somewhere on the seld. "Your mother must have moved it", I found it in a drawer but phoned her too. "We'll get a doctor and come up." You were so cold: I raked the ashes in the open grate, performing a daily task, talking to you.

Then you cried out to your mother, cried out to me and shook. Blood crimson, a violent wave of purple, moving to wax. An *Etch A Sketch* you wiped clear; face flooded from colour to blankness. "Come quick!" I screamed. I tried so many things, were my actions in the right order? Giving you a final kiss, still smelling of you. Offering you everything from my lungs, still against the dark, *breathe in breathe out* – willing my warmth into you. Ash on my fingers, happening too soon. I rang a neighbour who threw her army surplus coat over you, she'd never seen a dead body. A community told you she would have wanted it this way, a last kiss, being present, a gift.

56. Skin

Days, nights and evenings of long shifts to make money while you applied for jobs which led to a "career". The first mobile phone signified bondage to the agency, no glamour there.

The first night shift in a care home in Hove at short notice. A Georgian building spliced and rearranged, no longer making sense, corridors entering shared rooms built for dining, a tinny television sound in each room. Pads and incontinence sheets stacked on metal units. You were there to help men and women, once loved and held tenderly, whose limbs no longer worked; holes for mouths they had forgotten speech.

"What can I do in a day?", you ask yourself. No time between the moving of frail bodies in beds, a broken wing here, a purple blemish there, signs of a needle's entry on a hand. One of the skills learnt: how to change a bed while the person lay from immobility, ill health, or extreme pain. To do this without creating more pain, the ill would bellow. Checking the skin for breakages, beginnings of bedsores, the need for the sterile envelope called *Aquacel* never time to do things in the right order. The frustrating speed at which the elderly were bathed, changed, fed, bathed changed, fed. This was not your hometown, or your country, you tried not to rush those who could no longer move, to bathe them kindly and ensure you spoke even when they could not reply.

Your mother told you that hearing is the last to go. You tried not to chatter. The least you could tell Lily, Florence, Ruby, William and Johnny was that you were very sorry, but you had to move their left leg / right leg / left arm / right arm / left buttock / right buttock ensuring they were clean and safe.

Sometimes there were full names over the beds; although eyes were closed and they did not care where Princess Di was to be buried, whether Earl Spencer was a hero or how the flowers given to the queen of hearts were scooped up by a JCB, their stalks rotten. Formally addressing those in your care as Mr Wade, Miss Herbert, Mr Evans, Mrs Philpott as though you might be asking them their views on the general election, or the time while on your way to Trafalgar Square. Framed in that first day was the distress of your grandfather's return from respite care with pressure sores on his body. Such care your grandmother gave his manuscript skin, once held and loved at sixteen, swabbed and dusted.

57. Factory

You're in the workshop with the assembly line. You're sitting down. The line is going to start. Palpable air. Blank memory (Leslie Kaplan)

I was only in the factory once, very small without language. A man driving a forklift truck, fun in this enormous space, making it dance. Lights on, sun outside, the need for cold, butter cannot melt, milk cannot curdle. Movement around me stopped, the button paused a line of boxes.

The town known for its king: Hywel Dda, the unifying lawmaker from the tenth century, a good man, the town his senate. This factory is the main employer of this town, sheeted plastic, glass and metal already telling us "this is impermanence". Industrial buildings already forewarning us of closure: government development schemes that leave spaces of concrete, weeds breaking through.

But this is to write of a future, let me take you into the building. My father wearing a hair net under a pointed white cotton cap with *MMB* across its front. The *Milk Marketing Board* did a bit of everything in days when milkmen existed: rice pudding, butter, yoghurt, fruit juice. The men loved that moment of unscheduled break, a child's visit disrupting and disordering space. His alarm clock, shift work, small rituals punctuating dark mornings: it hurt to think of him working so early. Flush, electric shaver, cereal, first smoke, the car started and warmed on frosty mornings. The delicious delay.

As I got older and the learning harder, your rituals became my alarm. As your car left, I would finish drafts: an analysis of Pinter, Austen – beloved Pinter, loathsome Austen. I loved the stories of mini rebellions, the made objects, a steel and copper poker a semi-skilled fitter, using spent materials during breaktimes. In exasperation you would challenge the supervisor and tell him to sort out a broken machine and walk away. Or, the story of Prince Charles, to honour his visit your boss demanded that all the machinery was painted blue, the butter packing stalled, boxes fell.

58. Weight Watching

Warmth of bodies, the company of women, a summer's evening. Testing against the expectations of failure, for diabetes and health. The body turning upon itself, the rubbing thighs that hurt in this heat. A narrative of before and after, anecdotes of food, not as enemy but as the realisation of desire – an instant of gratification.

"Did we count our calories this week" asks the woman whose larger self stands in front of the class, a carboard cut-out in a seventies swimsuit with a big smile, dimpled arms and legs. "Did we count our carbs, proteins, free food our spectacular sins?" Women turning self-hatred to self-love. Acknowledging that joints, muscles, breasts need care. The despair of the teenage body, willing hardness felt in tightening the calves, upper arms, thighs, your chin tight.

Near firelight a child watches her grandmother, they count coins and notes together at the table. Curtains drawn, door locked nobody will ever see the coppers and silvers, turrets on the table. After the tally a treat from the shop. Deciding, the child is aware that *petits fours* in a white carboard box are reserved for an elderly lady. Once she peered into the stiff box at the pale flush of painted sweets. Smuggling the violet sweetness, coconut milk dribbled down the sides of her mouth. Days spent trying to recreate guilt's taste, crystallising violets and primroses in sticky sculptures, composted sugar. The woman lives in a stone longhouse with her daughter, they have a cane chair hanging chair from the rafters. Friends to her grandmother, both have silver buns. The grandmother likes independent women with independent incomes. Oh, the taste of that first bite, the sweet damask of the tongue bursting colour against the mouth's roof!

59. St David's

At fifteen you are interested in mental health; the school is encouraging pupils to gain experience of world beyond the self. Friends sit in surgeries watching animals being injected, arranging their food bowls each afternoon.

You volunteer for a week at the local psychiatric hospital named after the patron saint of Wales. The hospital on a hill visible from the snaking train into the town's station, Victorian stone. Unknown to you your grandfather died in one of the original locked wards. When you are older and impertinently ask, you find that your grandmother could not cope with his stroke since it led to violence. You learn about the difficulty of visiting him, having to close the village shop, placing two young children with neighbours, taking the bus journey to town and back. To be met by an even more violent husband demanding return, until the nurses urged her not to visit: it made the ward unbearable. The GP told her "stroke patients take out their frustrations on those they love most". Small comfort when you are punched in the face, facing your customers as the bruise goes from red to purple, green then finally yellow.

Your grandmother watched your morning departures: dungarees, a red handkerchief in your hair. The volunteer coordinator was a part-time minister known for his jet-black wig. Wiggy Watkins took down your details, offering too much eye contact, slight in a navy suit. You tried to ignore his stare across your body through black rimmed glasses. First morning, doors were locked after you. Led down the corridor, you saw the dining room and wanted to cry, women staring at their food, pools of gravy. Plastic bibs, *Velcro* fastening shoes, assistants carefully trying to spoon custard into women's mouths. That first day you told your grandmother "the women are imprisoned." One woman constantly looked for a way out. Walking up and down the ward chanting *Yukka yukka yukka yukka,* only pausing when she talked to Wiggy Watkins, who ignored the mouth that did not work.

60. Console

The trim phone might ring early evening, slender in its cradle. It became the enemy of family visits, mealtimes, its timing gave the phone personality. You didn't care too much about the rescheduling, and liked taking messages when your mother was unavailable. Voices often panicked or breathy at first not recognising that you were the child of a midwife and not *the* midwife. You were told things you recognised but did not understand: "My contractions are coming every five minutes", "my waters have broken". All physical conditions in textbooks stacked neatly under the telephone console. You might flick through *Physiology for Nurses* by Deryck Taverner, *The Preterm Baby and Other Babies with Low Birth Weight* by V. Mary Crosse. Your favourite was Derrek Llewelyn-Jones's *Fundamental of Obstetrics & Gynaecology* a cardinal red cover with speckled blobs for cells.

You looked at the images of women placed next to a measuring stick, eyes taped, their bodies bare. Graphs of disorders to the menstrual cycle: carcinoma of the cervix *menorrhoea* (the absence of menstruation) and *Oligomenorrhoea* (infrequent menstruations). You imagined the womb and cervix, the body's anarchy. You wondered at the multisyllabic words that underlined an abnormality. You found joy in the mispronunciation of their Latinate rhythms. New words for parts of your body visible only through dissection. Or, as Mr Llewelyn-Jones tells the story: the disorderly, dysfunctional anatomy that rebels against the charts and graphs. In the *sagittal* section of the pelvis the woman erect, the uterus sits waiting for new life in its bend, the bladder nuzzling the ovary.

In the early 80s more positive titles were added: *Birth Reborn: What a Birth Can and Should be* and *New Life*. Photos of women holding babies, cords still attached, fathers with beards smiling. Women with nipples like brown raspberries not giving a damn about the camera, their hair wet from a birth pool. Dialling home you would pretend to be one of your mother's pregnancies - would your father direct you to ambulance control, or pause to laugh and swear at you simultaneously?

61. Natality

Winter evening, your mother has taken over the kitchen table, calligraphy pens in red, green, yellow and black, rolls of paper. She sits sketching the curve of a woman's body, the full roundness of pregnancy. Above the curved line is the title BREAST IS BEST. Below is face of the mollusc baby. The poster gives the benefits of breastmilk, it shows how ducts are filled giving instruction. This poster will be placed in the small Laugharne surgery next to others warning against alcohol, one featuring a pregnant woman with a cigarette.

Decades later, you remember this evening of curves, tracing a line, the arrows on the woman's breast. You are in Dublin at a breast-feeding prenatal session with fourteen women. All shuffling their bottoms on hard chairs, trying to get comfortable. Thighs slightly apart. The first video, an Australian women breast feeding, clothes and hair dated, an emphatic positivity that grates. A box full of babies is passed around to cuddle. Then another box of knitted breasts, at first you think it is a mistake. Each breast is different, the size of the aureole shifts, nipple shape alert to race and difference, wool changes: damask pink, beige, arabesque, tanned brown. With light woollen breasts you are taught to express imaginary milk, no mention of mastitis. These teaching aids knitted by a nurse from a pattern, she varies the size and colour for credibility.

In your mother's kitchen, even the fridge became a pregnancy workshop. A small box with glass slides next to farm eggs. An early pregnancy kit for those wanting confidentiality in a small town. How natural it seemed, jam jars of urine of the back step, awaiting her return from a family gathering.

62. Mansions of Music

In "Ave Maria" Frank O'Hara asks the *Mothers of America* to send their kids to the movies. He reasons that in so doing they will not get stuck at home "hating you prematurely". Had O'Hara lived to see the 1980s, and was Welsh speaking, these lines would have been updated: Mothers of Wales let your daughters go to *Cymdeithas yr Iaith* gigs.

1980's West Wales had an ambivalent relationship to the language; bilingual education an experiment, English language music was king. When you went to the new bilingual school, in a wool striped tunic you were taunted "Welsh Nash" and "hambone." Such was the cultural self-hatred in that part of the world. Pupils transitioned from a ska / post-punk to a Welsh language music dominated by cock rock. From 1982-5 Welsh language music was masculine and hairy. Unappealing to a teenager with glamorous posters of lithe men wearing make-up, tense with vivid sexuality. Their artfully painted faces reflected little of life in West Wales.

When you were fourteen, older students started a political newsletter *Brych ecs Collwyn ap Tango,* a title which became more convoluted during its history. Info about *Cymdeithas'* political campaigns, music reviews and gig listings. Through an animal rights compilation EP *Dyma'r Rysait* (1987) you encountered Datblygu, Crisialau Plastig, Plant Bach Ofnus and Eirin Peryglus. The iconoclastic nature of Datblygu's vignette "Brechdanau Tywod", a schoolteacher's boast about eating snails in Brittany. Bands that linked Welsh idiom to creativity and not atrophy. The cheap LED clock radio opened you to John Peel's listening community. You copied tapes from other initiates of synths and guitar noise: Y Cyrff – *Dan y Cownter* (*Under the Counter*), Anhrefn – *Defaid, Skateboards a Wellies,* Traddodiad Ofnus' biography of post-industrial South Wales and Ffa Coffi Pawb's hymn to valium in *Dalec Peilon.* The relationship between Peel's programme and Welsh music has been well parsed. But oh the impact of those *Cymdeithas* gigs away from a metropolis! Gigs in country mansions turned rural hotels, out of the way community centres and village halls. Freedom to experiment, we were heavy on the eyeliner, clothes, backcombing our fringes, dreaming the republic.

63. Dada in Pontardawe

You are watching your favourite band Datblygu sampling a hairdryer. David R. Edwards is making the audience wait, sound looped back to the synthesizer creating the backing track for "Cristion yn y Kibbutz". It has taken persuasion to get here, a road off the M4 to Swansea. Zipping past new industrial estates (post miners' strike), opened by a Conservative Minister in the Welsh Office, flanked by Labour councillors.

Too young to drive, too young to drink, your friend's sister agreed to chauffeur you to a community centre in Pontardawe. Screams of laughter, twice round a roundabout: you reflect on how young women arrange events, but never play. Preparing for gigs is cabaret, taking up the hem on 60s psychedelia, marshalling the confidence of a red plastic mac. Or, borrowing a father's choir tux, before vintage became a knowing word. No mention of cigarette smoke or whiskey breath on the pickup.

This experiment is part of the fabric of keeping Welsh *contemporary*. Datblygu pen a song "Bar Hwyr" ("Late Bar") to taunt a hostile, drunken audience. Dadaism and anarchy: the pertinent challenge to a respectability haunting Welsh culture. Finding albums requires research, you explore music through political pamphlets, posting your SAEs with Liz's head upside down. During 'O' level revision the doorbell rings, "a friend" is ushered in, it is Pat, Datblygu's bassist on her way to Thomas's Boathouse delivering an LP. Shyly, you both sit on the patio, trying to find words to tell how much music means. Dark humour against raw guitar and insistent keyboards, how you chant on a daily basis: "Rwy'n teimlo fel *Cymdeithas yr Iaith*, neu dyn dall yn chwilio am waith."‡

Testing these assertions against your tongue. Reviews in the *NME* littered with analogies to Tom Jones and male voice choirs, but music's allusions open up a new archive. Anger as bassline in Public Image Ltd, ludic riposte in The Fall, combative drone in The Jesus and Mary Chain, lyrics as agitation for Patti Smith. That shift from the solitary *I* to a shared possibility born in the language you love.

---

‡ Translates as "I feel like the Welsh Language Society/or a blind man seeking work."

64. Lecturing the Young

In her early twenties she wondered how does the self-relate to other selves? Her friend tells her about Plato's *Symposium* the split self in search of its partner, an ideal of good forms created through union. Not a suturing, but the indelible beauty of unification, the philosopher who taught the Plato class was so emphatic, that he cried. In its retelling, she felt her friend's sad pleasure, the description of the man's dark eyes full of tears. A form of teaching not encountered before.

Others were more daring in testing out their selves through pedagogical relationships. This was the '90s, her friends felt that they could handle themselves. Pretending their narrative was from Françoise Sagan's *Bonjour Tristesse*. Challenging the men that stood articulating random thoughts at lecterns. For some, liaisons continued after their degrees, transatlantic departure rooms, conferences, visits to retreats. For others the lecturers who wanted to be lovers pursued them through home addresses, demanding contact. Using the power of *their* language, their power. One student thought she adored a married man. His stare had made her self-conscious, he had praised her for emphasising *cunt* in her reading of *that* poem by Derek Mahon. Deliberately *shocking* and *misogynistic*: now she had the answer. A naked grin now abhorrent to her, she had thought this man witty, interested in her scholarship. Later he panicked phoning her studio apartment. She blushed crimson, his desire had become sequential clichés. Staring at the squares of green stiff carpet, the bed that folded into a wall, her cassette copy of *To Bring you my Love* and PJ Harvey's sculpted face. She responded quietly "No I am working that day, this is not a good idea."

65. Three True Objects

The writing slope was given a century ago to a woman who wrote letters with a fountain pen, blotting carefully in case words spilled. An eyelash caught the nib, making an inky flower at the centre of a letter to a soldier far from home.

A century before we generate daily text, wrapping the world in dactylic strophes. Erasure once meant time to start again, to make lucid the duration of a sentence. Or, maybe these are all untruths. The slope closes, forming a polished rosewood box missing its mother of pearl inlay. In its new home, three things that are true are hidden in the slope's leather incline.

The first is a small pink parcel of Peter Rabbit wrapping paper. A parcel so small that all one sees is Peter's ears and nose. Opened many times, the Sellotape has crackled and dried. In the parcel is small plastic clamp with the intact and leathery stub of a baby's cord.

Next is a velvet bag for costume jewellery, drawn shut but opens easily. Purple tissue paper protects a small white stick, a ribbon looped at its top. A carved ivory baby's teether from the 19th Century given by two gentle antique dealers. She is worried about displaying it, her daughter points to elephants in magazines, asking "why are bad people killing them?"

The third is a handkerchief framed with a border of red, white and blue neatly ironed. Owned by a mother whose work was sustenance and song her gift, the laundry smell, an imprint. Its owner taught her how to make wasps suffer in summer. The instructions were simple: *Slit the lid of an empty Robinson's jam jar, fill the base with water, smear the lid with jam and screw back on, place on wall.* The wasps filed into the jar, delighting, failing to return they flew till exhausted and drowned, the sound of others did not deter.

66. Fortified

You watch T's face as the headteacher accidently kicks the plastic bag next to the desk: a clink. T looks at you: he has started telling you things. You sit beside one another in the headmaster's classroom; the toughest kid in primary school. Punching, pinching, teaching boys to give love bites, a big beautiful grin on his face.

Your mother has complained about Welsh language provision in the school, your spoken Welsh has deteriorated to a rusty anglicised *bratiaith*. That word has its own connotations: dirty, useless, a language sullied, in bits, rendered fragmentary. In time, Welsh language campaigners will scorn the term stating no hierarchy should exist to shame speakers in non-Welsh speaking areas. There has been a failed devolution referendum, the language will not survive if education offers no care. You and two best friends are moved to the upper class, here the headmaster prepares pupils for the eleven plus, another anachronism. An examination that the education board will cling to for many years.

T and the two other boys are in this classroom since they find reading difficult. In T's plastic bag are four bottles of fortified beer – *Gold Label*, T bought them in the grocer's near the school, telling the owner they were for his father. His father works in Pendine's MOD "Establishment", a military weapons development site, loading rockets on to cradles for testing underground. Later, it will be privatised, *Qinetic* will take over much of ballistic testing in Wales, the workers returned in buses each night. T's father beats his wife and the kids, except the girls. He tells you about his older brother putting cushions into both their pyjamas before their father returns from the pub. This makes the father even angrier.

That evening T will throw up in the bus on the way back from swimming. You associate the brand with a gentle alcoholic woman who buys bottles from your grandmother's shop, and is routinely beaten by her husband.

67. Viva H. Samuel

In your writing, try not to reduce the children you knew to stereotype: council estates with wild families, no capital, coin slots for electricity, gas and tv. In the entrepreneurial eighties, she followed her mother in and out of homes, invites to *Tupperware* and jewellery parties. One jewellery party meant looking at catalogues with a *Babycham* or *Lambrusco* served from the little bar in the corner. The bar fascinated her, a work of art bevelled with mirror mosaics, an indoor awning with optic stands and gold cocktail sticks. Behind the bar was a large Elvis clock. In his white jumpsuit he turned his hips right, she preferred him in denim jacket and jeans testing the throttle of his motorbike on a wall of death.

Her mother must buy something at this party: the hostess had her second child two months ago. "Have you seen anything you might like" she whispers, they are both in long viscose maxi dresses. There is a silver metallic cat poised on a small circle with a stiff tail that can hold rings, but having only one ring, it serves little purpose. She points to the silver hedgehog charm on a thin chain. Some years later the girl, now a woman who has given up animal charms, will meet a primary school friend T as a customer. She works in a jewellery store while looking for a "career" in Wales. Early 90s she loves her town but there is little on offer; petrol and parking eats her part time pay, she scans the *Western Mail* and develops her profile.

T comes in with a grin and a natty moustache, it is Christmas he is getting engaged, an eagle tattoo on his neck against the collar of his leather jacket. He had been in prison for stealing: BBC Wales reported he tried to commit suicide. The item called for more resources and support in Wales's Victorian prisons. He looks better than the pale photo on the TV screen, but he makes her nervous asking for trays of diamonds, she fumbles with the keychain, the sliding glass of display cabinets. She keeps him talking, feels she can trust him once they share stories about primary school, the kids they mutually disliked. It is not a day for successful ring buying "Good to see you" T winks. A song from a passing car tells her of another time when everybody wore parkas and round toed creepers at discos: *Pass the blame and don't blame me — just close your eyes and count to three.*

68. First Language

Upstairs the child listens to the conversation below. She situates the voices next to the kettle between table and stove. Her grandmother sits, the mother talks with force. "I felt embarrassed listening, her friends have better Welsh, better than my child." Listening, the child feels the red blush creeping on her neck.

Her friends, originally from Sussex, attend the local school and have sucked the language through invisible gills. The mother goes on: "The school is useless; her language is so poor." The grandmother's voice tries to be reassuring, but the child hears a tone of terrible doubt. She knows this is trouble; if her grandmother pities her, all is lost. Poems once memorised can be performed publicly in harmony with language. It is the impromptu, when she is asked a question her sounds are false, she is busily translating phrases into another language. This language with its precocious sound structures, loses accuracy in her mouth. She has never played in the language; her best friends turn to English: now she wonders whether this is to accommodate *her*.

It is a deep trouble this language, the weekend terrifying. Trying to write Welsh composition on "My Weekend" she cannot conjugate the verbs. Her mother screamed at her grammar, the child's colour drained. Anger, recrimination, linguistic failure becoming a fatal human flaw, her legs almost buckle, she stands looking at a fly speck on the wallpaper. A high pitched humming returns, her silence seeming to aggravate. Her father running asking what was wrong. And the mother sobbing in the bathroom, looking at her red eyes in the mirror "I could kill her, her language."

69. Is There a Penis in the House?

Music warned you of slick presenters, the sheen on their faces, the easy words, making money from a minority language, far from the world you inhabited. A different Welsh, a self-appointed guardianship refuting tattered or evolved expression, a club for initiates on the small screen. As a child you smelt the carbolic soap and borax emanating from male bodies, folded into permanent pressed trousers.

You thought about the political situation for days, talking with a husband and friends, following an invitation to speak on TV. You arrive, full of translated political phrases, ready for business, waiting for war paint. The make-up artist tells you about the island, the devastation at knowing the nuclear power station they had spent years trying to attract, has been scrapped. Hastily you articulate your concern about Wales as a playground for the MOD. The private companies operating ballistic testing in West Wales. She looks at you with no anger "my husband is a fighter pilot in Valley, this is what we have here." Deftly brushing under eye, closing your lid, you look up for mascara, she powders the gap between your neck and chest to avoid a line, she was kind. Between blusher, eyeliner and highlighter you talked about small villages, bigger towns, closed shops, the large supermarkets that stalked in square kilometres.

Exchanging stories, how once people congregated to talk and laugh and fight over politics, over love in your language. Companies came with boasts of jobs, councils facilitated offering planning and no business rates. She tells you her mother could not buy chocolates from the wholesaler at the price the supermarket sold, "Game Up". Wearing mascara, blusher, foundation, powder with backcombed hair you realise that things have not changed in the country that you love.

The presenter looks in, mouthing hello, wanting to be seen, a bead of sweat on his forehead. You are torn, Welsh has become your language of compassion, care, restitution, a language of reconciliation. Not the language of argument, outmanoeuvring, polysyllabic words that wind, dazzle and explode against your tongue. In the blood beat of the ear you hear the music of your past: scraping metal, industrial sounds punctuated by the breakbeat of a synthesiser. As the politicians arrive for their makeup, you understand you are gender window dressing, a dated exile, pebbles in your mouth.

70. Speaking for Oneself (in the Nation)

A practice question and cameras roll, the set is hot: halogen lights bounce against the sheet metal of the harbour atrium. The woman who now lives in another language is on this panel because she is worried about fascism, how migrants and asylum seekers are depicted in the populist press. Language games, the play of reformation around a "backstop". This story could be how a once prosperous, resource-hungry empire became a dwindling world economy and wanted to gain back a word – "sovereignty".

It is too warm, she needs space from the earnest young conservative panellist who keeps telling her about car journeys with his parents. In the bathroom with a full face of make-up, her eyes large, an audience member approaches her. They talk about where she has travelled from, the heat on set: she pointedly notes, "They did not use my question about Shamima Begum". The woman too had prepared for a question concerning the fifteen year old girl who travelled to ISIS in Syria, the girl had buried two children and birthed a third in a refugee camp. No secret that they are given the questions two hours in advance: "It is important to address, our history in this war," she mumbles. They smile awkwardly.

She walks back to the green room, screened by a pot plant, there an ex-political officio speaks about Welsh dialect, he is jovial, a machine of witticism and jibes. Another man, a member of the Assembly, stands calmly half listening as Mr Ex-officio speaks with a dark haired community activist, they finish one another's sentences. The politicos turn to one another sharing a nickname, a flash of recognition, a transaction occurs. The presenter re-enters: "Don't start becoming friends, I need some boxing tonight." In that moment the woman knows her fate, a spectacle, she lacks rhetorical determination and has never loved data.

It takes the chair fifteen minutes (with an ad break) to accept an interjection from her; she has stared at him intently for five minutes, made a note of his mole, his thinning hair. The question is one about a referendum, the future of a country "desiring its sovereignty" and in annoyance she spits out: "*Cambridge Analytica* – do we actually know who owns the last referendum?" Members of the audience begin to clap, the elderly woman wearing a woollen dress and small beret, the young goth, the woman with a Clash T shirt and a man who looks like Sydney Greenstreet. The presenter turns to her and flashes a smile, "Thank you for that, now on to our next question." A man from the audience asks "Was this island naïve to rely on foreign investment in a nuclear power station to solve our unemployment?" and the presenter's brow furrows, but the camera's red light turns to Mr Ex-officio once more.

71. Plastic Passion

This year there is music in your house, your parents move awkwardly to disco beats. Careful in crimplene and long polyester dresses, shiny shoes and ruffled shirts. Lurex on the TV, the body in plastic, you drink from melamine mugs, your nightdress crackles against sheets.

Two years before "Video Killed the Radio Star", two years after Abba's "SOS" you have fallen in love with Elvis Presley. At six you curate your wardrobe to match the Elvis film on Saturday TV. The deep red embroidery of a rose on at tight denim jacket, watching him in *Roustabout* on a Honda 350 Super Hawk. Forty years before you find how broken Elvis became, Hawaiian shirts in Technicolor, he tinkered with engines, songs which seemed spontaneous. His sneer, hair, hips, oil on his hands mirroring your uncle working in a homemade car inspection pit. Shovelled from earth with no joists he hit the riverbed, it flooded and crumbled.

That year you were happy to be taken for a boy, you wanted to walk like a boy, bouncing long strides on the pavement. Friendships with boys meant violence on the playground: running fast, colliding into bodies, hair pulled, bruises became badges. Until four boys were taken to the headmaster for the dap, a black plimsoll. They had given one another love bites; you did not fully understand but knew it inappropriate.

Like the secret shared that summer with a ten-year-old girl. Your mothers were exchanging district nurse duties: a woman homeless in a shelter, supporting the aged, the lonely. "Come here," she commanded obediently you did; she held a jar – a small creature inside. "Don't tell," she whispered. "The mother doesn't know we have her baby," she slipped the bobbing foetus back under the sink between *Emo* washing powder and *Brillo* scouring pads. You are only reminded of this moment when Esther Greenwood tells us in *The Bell Jar*, "I liked looking on at other people in crucial situations. If there was a road accident or a street fight or a baby pickled in a laboratory jar for me to look at, I'd stop and look so hard I never forgot it."

72. Careering

Newly graduated, early 1990s applying for jobs in Wales, she writes letters in alliterative sentences. The young woman sits a translator's exam in the hope of getting work in S4C's commissioning office and scores her worst grade since a school sewing assignment.

Every day the postman sits at the table for his toast and marmalade, while her grandmother makes tea and passes the wad of rejections. It becomes their ritual, the postman offering slight envelopes, waiting for the weekly appointments page, things moved less frenetically but left traces of language on one's fingers.

"How long is a 17 inch chain" the earnest man asked in the jewellery shop. The public moved her, the worried farmers with their pocketbooks looking for jewellery on Christmas Eve. "Would you wear this?" they ask pointing to a diamante necklace with enamel roses. Sombre wives enter before New Year, scrubbed nails and red rough hands, to exchange the "rose set" for a plain gold chain.

She knew a little dub poetry, some language writing and was familiar with recent debates over the lyric, she wondered whether customer care was her calling. The intricacies of knowing the right key for any cabinet, the reverent hush which follows a tray of diamond rings. Upstairs gesticulating to co-workers from a chair: "The great Welsh public want to be told what to like, to make the right choice." Three years from a referendum that offers devolution, this small town with its jewellery shops, ancient coffee pot above its square, a large hat as signage for a gent's outfitters, will push the nation over the line.

A letter she thought that might never arrive comes from the postman, an interview for a job in an archive of voices. She thinks of the archives she has visited, two in California, the whirr and scrape of tape is part of retrieval. The night before the interview she dreams of a position in "the cabinet of sound" she mistook *Zebra* grate polish for *Kiwi*-her boots are now so Ziggy Stardust. "Check the record, check the record, check the guy's track record" sings Mark E. Smith in her ear the moment she is asked how institutions work. She offers the NHS; is knowledgeable about the different hip replacements she encountered as an auxiliary. Later she is escorted to the personnel office to fill a claim form, there stands her former history teacher filling in the same paperwork. They share the train back to their town. She tells him about adventures in American poetry, he tells her about working as the editor of the newspaper for the blind.

73. Cŵl Cymru

So much of your teenage years was spent waiting: counting days, planning, moving towards something as yet unknowable, waiting for "something to happen". Bus stops were spaces of the imagination, smoking and the possibilities of sexual awakening.

Curled up on your boyfriend's bed listening to Japan's 'Ghosts', in the dark you both try to pinpoint the moment that David Sylvian's voice cracks into something more than singing. Play and rewind, play and rewind, guess the song's time curve through touch of the controls, the spool's screech is part of the listening. He tries to emulate the intricacy of the soundscape on his keyboard, in front of a window overlooking a level crossing. But always ends up with the riff from "Love will Tear Us Apart" against the sound of a passing train reminding you of Depeche's "Somebody".

While you admire your boyfriend, his challenge to a small town, making himself the target of ridicule, you recognise he makes no space for your Welsh indie music, or language. You admired him for daring to bleach his hair, this is how you first knew him, from a distance. You were attracted to the way he walked, loping across pavements and studied him from your parents' bungalow. He is as far from agriculture as you can possibly get. Your best friend had a crush on him and wrote his name on her pencil case with glitter glue, which you thought "adolescent". You studied him for years, this boy from the grammar school who looked like he hated everything, in your notebook you write *nihilist* in five different colours followed by his name.

The night you met you had not wanted to go to the lousy nightclub, with its sticky floor, chart music and rising tide from the Tywi, the only hope was that the 12 inch of "Tainted Love" would get played – *Baby Baby where did our love go*? That Saturday you cleaned up an old workman's lamp at your grandmother's, your friends came over, you smelt of pink paraffin, a taste like metal in your mouth. What you wear is so important: tonight you have no choice except for a recently dyed graphic dress that was given in a charity shop bag. With your school cardigan and shoes, an old green mac with a hole in the pocket, eyeliner, white foundation and backcombed fringe you are persuaded into their car. That night you see him, he saw you for the first time; since you are not driving you are drinking, his hunger hits your stomach – you walk towards him. Trading insults about the music, a quizzical conversation ends with his mouth pressed onto yours, holding hands in a nightclub that plays Kylie Minogue. The immediacy of it – he'll arrive at your doorstep for your first proper date with eyeliner, snarled red lipstick, black leather trousers under his ripped jeans with *Reebok* Hi Tops. Your father gently attempts small talk showing him recently planted apple trees, while you slide yourself into black shiny tights.

74. Oilskins

A small man on a bicycle chases your grandmother over a bridge into a field, she always wakes up before he catches her. You see poverty daily, but have no words for what you see. Unwashed men with stubble, in cut down coats, driving battered cars, their hats greasy, hair prematurely grey. No belts, orange plastic baler twine, some are benign, others malign. Some are so used to no company they struggle for language; words are small grunts, some are misers, others hungry.

Now you can offer comparisons to Caradoc Evans, his modernist grotesques, how cleanliness is next to godliness made people strain even when outdone by labour. You are small, sit with your grandmother meeting customers, watching her put groceries on tab in coloured copy books. You are told of one customer you loved as a child, a middle aged man who rode a Chopper bike, a plastic bag over the split seat. He smelled of oilskins, old sweat and hay. "Then suddenly you stopped kissing his face and hugging him." You remember a red stool and seeing something long and fleshy poking out from his trousers which he pointed at. He asked you to take your knickers off, you ran.

Oilskin man became infatuated with the widow who ran a post office. He stalked her, knowing her daily routine. One day he refused to leave, howling outside her shop until the police took him away. In your recurring dream a poet puts on ceremonial robes of purple and gold. His face is gentle as he touches your knee kindly (this dream is not about desire), and whispers in Welsh that he must leave. Your voice reduced to a croak, soon you will have to address an impatient crowd. The narrative requires that you must find water and vinegar to unclench your throat which is burning. The only word you hear is *Phil-o-men-a*, broken to syllables, fighting in phonemes.

75. The Labour of Language

Everyone in your family works hard, not from protestant fanaticism or the delirium of profit, they have no choice. Everyone is fine with working hard, until they see what they hold dear ridiculed by others. Or, the ignorance of those who have never balanced one language against another.

The well-intentioned, point to the sweet bottles in your grandmother's shop and whisper *quaint*. Or speak very slowly after you'd asked her (in your language): "Where are these people from? Do you need help?" You wince as they comment aloud: the absence of a cash register, the *Avery* scale, paper and not plastic bags, the cheese unrefrigerated on its cold slab, the pump has no coupons since the petrol is *BECA*.

You are surrounded by people who work hard, your father in a factory when he should have been sculpting hedges and talking to birds. He does not tell you how the roll of tins, cheese and butter require constant care, the machines demand the life of this man who needs open air. The movement of conveyor belts, the tins, boxes and hot glue make him anxious until the beat falls counter the body, counter the heart. Nobody knows this yet, in spite of his getting into a car an hour too early, the fear of not being *on time*. Until the machines win their bet against the heart's rhythm: the man who should have worked in the open air falls on the cement floor. Working hard, *arrhythmia* an illness, he retires ill.

There are few jobs, most relate to the diurnal pattern of birthing, milking and slaughter. No romance to hard work, there *is* only hard work. Your grandmother would chuckle at being sent the fortnightly *Asian Trader* through the post and tap the subtitle *Convenience Store* knowingly. A sign to her that other cultures shared labour, serving the convenience of others. The shop of an old woman with bandages on her legs, opening late because somebody forgot eggs in the supermarket, wanted a spare loaf, or ran out of petrol and honked their horn at midnight.

In a dream, you serve petrol, the feel of the heavy bulb in your palm; as you train its hook upwards, the machine comes to life. You have painted its metal case many times, anticipated the weights & measures inspector. But of late, you are rough with the nozzle as it clicks to full and spits over a visitor's watered silk blouse, offering a new pattern.

76. C90: Boxes of Culture

You realise that being a female music obsessive renders you a minority. Add to this being a music obsessive of Welsh language post-punk music. Knowing the lyrics and transition from album to album is shared by few teenage girls.

Young women organise political benefits, gigs that generate new sounds to a generation of speakers who had their pop broadcast from London. The eroticism of the mix tape, how it tells of love unsaid. To show you care, an album of your own with a soundtrack of subtexts. Tracks in ironic counterpoint become a fixture in the mixtapes you receive, why not have "Sheela-Na-Gig" next to "Kinky Boots"? Welsh language records love intertextual irony: Crumblowers nod to Solzhenitsyn and John Heartfield's photo montages; *Gadael yr Ugeinfed Ganrif* [§] a wink to the Situationist's manifesto, Y Fflaps riffing a name from The Slits. This knowledge is as yet unknown, but will greet you in the future.

What could be better than a situationist revival in Wales, a parallel chronology to Manchester's Haçienda which since it did not exist "had to be built"? Abandoned slate quarries become venues for colour and percussion, a raving utopia. A pursuit of pleasure in amphitheatres of industrial decay. The labour of factory work reflected in the boilersuits worn by ravers, loading lighting from a van. This new yet unapproachable Wales fielded in the DIY covers of cassette covers, posted to friends, would be lovers getting known, never famous.

Tired of reading the *NME, Melody Maker,* there is no witness to a braver Wales in the words? She swore never to buy a greatest hits album. So many small boxes carried, stuffed into rucksacks, taken on ferries, forced into envelopes, pictures glued on the front, hear the stylus jump, the click of a machine. Sharing, building, making, loving the language a spit in the eye, pogo jumping in darkness, anarchy in kindness, the breathy silt of vowels in your mouth. You shout, scream and preen in anger never hate; coming to punk in Welsh. Exorcism in the head, a hope that culture is *not* a war to be won.

[§]   trans *Leaving the Twentieth Century*

77. Extreme Listening

I want you to smile with this young woman: might there be an affinity between you and her? She needs understanding, wants you to read beyond the tropes of religiosity which straddle the language she inhabited daily. Until the language inhabited her, growing inside.

She made a truce with misspellings, botched conjugations and failing mutations. She searched for an answer to the question about her small country with its own language. Does all writing about community become about the trials that small communities engender? Her writing is an attempt towards encountering the problem: she cannot dissect in a language that does not to love her mouth. But the language grew remarkable inside, gently from follicle to breathing cell. An organ, then a limb, the bubble of eyes, a spine sharpened, nickel in the dark. She carried this knowledge inside her, not as martyrdom but as power.

This woman who had begun to love her language, walks into a hall at a prestigious institution, where two men speak to an audience about British-ness, politics and music. One an avant-garde poet dressed as a skateboarder, asks questions of a journalist who will later become a columnist on Brexit. The importance of not liking Coldplay, is iterated at many points, to knowing laughs, a punctuation point. Being in an audience, in a body with language growing inside her, its limbs and bent head expectant. She listens attentively to their discussion, the narrative of punk, telling many things she has heard: late nights the flicker of familiar documented images. The references are male, and she is tired of the verbal winks and laughs inscribed in their exchange – its *performed knowingness*.

During Q&A the language inside her makes her ask about the Mercury prize and PJ Harvey's *Let England Shake* a title with relevance to their talk. They begin smiling, words are pats on the head, until the language inside makes words that snip and grimace "I am so tired of hearing men talk about punk as if they invented it themselves"– silence. Slowly women in the audience add to the conversation, the need to think more about dub, trip hop, what the fuck is British-ness and a neat narrative falters. The swelling in her body tells her they are threatened and unlistening, but it is always she who blushes on their behalf.

78. On Not Knowing Osi Rhys Osmond

He is as yet unknown to her on the train back to the small town, delayed they start talking. The connecting journey missed, the cold platform, which she has known in attempts to see poets from afar. The privatisation of the railways is imminent but is yet to happen. Journeys are still honoured in ways that enable the passenger to arrive faster than the timetable, since a taxi is called. She speaks with the certainty of a twenty-year-old who knows what to do (how quickly that security dissipates).

They may have shared the book titles during the taxi ride to the small town. By this time the woman is accustomed to strange journeys, bags disappearing, over-anxious conversations about being from a smaller country, what it means to be travelling into a light that frames moments of inconsolable lucidity, grasped at and of course, lost.

Decades later in the small town she encounters an exhibition *Hawk and Helicopter.* "Is it Iraq or Afghanistan", she looks at the Chinook slicing up spaces along the Bay. Filleting the sky with its hardware; a swallow and hawk fly magnified by a watching lens. Verdigris fading, moving from scarlet to mauve and bleeding a uterine pink, the arc of a low-lying sun hits the water. An inscription in the small town she knows the artist loved.

In that moment, although it may be nostalgic to speak of epiphanies, it is not about the air or the light that wraps itself around night lengthening like yarn. She is there, knowing the military testing in the bay, the rocket sleighs underground, under fine sand, well after the land speed record of John Parry-Thomas, beyond the once buried Babs. The Leyland buses that picked up hard drinking men to work on the site when it was MOD, the headaches mentioned to district nurses which later became growths (never data to prove anything). Letters to the editor that missile testing was affecting the milk production of Friesians grazing near dotted sage, rounded wintergreen and petal wort. Making the pastoral work for arms investors. Moving the canvas to more than commentary, the compulsion to tend the sky and herd the hawk from danger. In the horizon hawk and helicopter are synonymous, occupying space. Death stars reflected onto the periwinkled pools, communicating with the speeded-up satellites in a Llansteffan day.

79. Facing It

Two aerial images exist, separated by forty years placed on a wall to create continuity and discontinuity. Similar to those on polished cupboards in farmhouses showing squat houses, concrete walkways, fields with black and white Friesians. Photographs that map out the importance of hedges and the maintenance of property. Machinery flattened into landscape. Travelling salesmen came infrequently, but every farm has one image displaying particular zeitgeists: orange cars, fluted yellow petrol pumps, limewashed walls, churn letterboxes, tractors with small tyres.

The salesman died: his family found thousands of photos, in boxes marked according to year. Maybe they were too expensive to those with little land, only a garden with peas and potatoes. Who wants a photograph of a home not their own in an age of drones and digital mapping? Ill at ease with a bonfire of images, his son follows the b roads his father took, offering vintage images of homes. He comes to our door and offers a photo that is forty years old. The photograph waits for revolution, a summer's day, doors and windows open, begonias on the windowsills. Singing carried by the river, arias while mopping a concrete shop floor.

It is so easy to buy into nostalgia, the taste of cherryade, the possibilities of rayon against your skin. Hush now, breathe easier, allow the encounters of that decade. You open a bedroom door of your friend's house and find her parents writhing on the bed bumping against one another. Later you find the father's mags and feel the warmth in your vagina, a new sort of hurt as you giggled at the readers' wives. It might be the story of a nine-year old friend who came to stay a night, no parent was home, she was terrified of social services. The casual racism of that decade, its sexism, anarchy, you now understand how a culture marks your breathing, etches your DNA. Ghosts leaving this village, abandoned the language, affecting accents exhausting the ear, slippages, a minefield of grammar and mispronunciation. Perhaps there is no error only attempts at affirmation; no failure but the redefining of identity; you gild the still but enquiring face, leaf by leaf.

80. The Waistcoat

Poetry was the wrong art for people who love justice. It was not like dance music –
Anne Boyer

Violence inscribed in a garment, the tale of making, blood soiled, lessons of being home, awaiting terror from the tyrant. Inside the binding of seams are stains of sweat, a high-pitched buzz sutured in thread. Confrontation generates a loop in the body, your face flushed, look directly ahead, features neutral and inert.

At sixteen you embrace an old man's waistcoat found hanging in a wardrobe smelling of dust and insects. Its multiple pockets allow you to carry keys and money, offering spaces of freedom, you pretend independence. Self-possession is what you seek, unknowing you have this already. A hidden pocket hides the stub of a pencil, the possibilities of words as yet unwritten. A faded green Rizla packet, FIVE LEAVES LEFT. The garment remained hidden for years, the remnant of a patriarch who bit his way through the world, speech stopped by a stroke.

Books remain: correspondence classes, guides to building motor engines, a treatise on what a husband might expect from a wife. Library of facts, contemplation through music, copies of anthems and a Latin primer, religion and matrimonial guides. "The one true and only test which any man should look for is modesty in demeanour before marriage, absence of both assumed ignorance and a disagreeable familiarity, and a pure and religious frame of mind." A grandmother responds to exhausting questions: "I burnt his letters of early love."

Waistcoat as talisman, worn through countries, over dresses, at interviews, at funerals, repossessed (you thought). Until it tightens, seams impinge the post-pregnancy body, breasts rub against the striped fabric, more brace than a becoming. Patterns of interrogation, witness the violence of white anger. A binding that marshals pain, breaking a cycle in Autumn, tree on pane. A day spent listening to the interpretations of poems, colleagues with problems, strategic planning, shoulders stiffened by a waistcoat restricting each gesture. The door closes easily on the fire, fuels a hologram, a chest burning to black cinder, holding its shape breathing in and out. Wind tearing through the cavity, leaving only a steel buckle, once harnessed to silk.

Acknowledgements

Some of the poems in *Republic* were published in the following journals *Poetry Wales*, *Planet*, *Junction Box*, *Icarus* and *Blackbox Manifold*. Many thanks to the support of their editors.

Sincere thanks to former Seren editor Amy Wack for her belief in the project and all the unwavering support from editors Zoë Brigley and Rhian Edwards (with the Seren team). I am also tremendously grateful to Pure Evil (Charles Uzzell Edwards) for his generous permission to use his artwork for the cover.

There are many kind writers, editors, institutions, artists, political thinkers and musicians who supported the writing of *Republic* in its various forms over the years. Sioned Rowlands, Angharad Penrhyn Jones, John Goodby, Lyndon Davies (Glasfryn Project), Peter Finch, Nia Davies, Emily Trahair, David Greenslade, *Llenyddiaeth Cymru* and *Passa Porta* in Brussels. A debt of gratitude to Pat Morgan and Rhys Mwyn for reading the ms and simply *being* in the Welsh musical landscape. I am also grateful for the time and care taken by Menna Elfyn and Gwyneth Lewis in reading the final draft. Thanks to important discussions had in Wales with Gaynor, Emyr Llew, Eiris, Kathleen (& Bill). As ever thanks to Sally, Yoshie, Michelle, Sue and Sarah for the conversation that supported writing.

Without the post-punk music of Wales in the 80s there would be no *Republic*. Thanks to all those musicians who travelled down B roads to play gigs in small venues with little recompense, who battled the mainstream with such humour. Their creativity made Welsh a pulsing and tangible language. In particular RIP David R. Edwards the acerbic-genius-wordsmith who made so many love *Cymraeg*.

And finally in Ireland to Myles and Gwyneth Owen (who continue to dance and sing in the kitchen once the needle touches vinyl).

Discography (by section number)

8

Elfyn Presli "Jackboots Maggie Thatcher" *The First Cuts Are The Deepest* (Words of Warning, 1987)

10

Grace Jones *Island Life* (Island, 1985)
Talking Heads "Psycho Killer" *Talking Heads: 77* (Sire, 1977)

11

David Bowie "I can't give everything away" *Blackstar* (Columbia, 2016)

12

Sex Pistols "God Save the Queen" *Never Mind the Bollocks: Here's The Sex Pistols* (Virgin, 1977)
The Cure "The Top" *The Top* (Fiction, 1984)

13

my bloody valentine "only shallow" *loveless* (Creation, 1991)
Joy Division "She's Lost Control" *Unknown Pleasures* (Factory, 1979)

15

Ludovicio Einaudi "Nuvole Blanche" *Una Mattina* (Sony, 2004)
Ludovicio Einaudi "Fuori Dal Mondo" *Eden Roc* (Sony, 1999)

19

Frank Sinatra "Theme from New York, New York" *Trilogy: Past Present Future* (Reprise, 1980)

22

Beatles "Help!" *Help!* (Parlaphone, 1965)
Val Doonican *Val Doonican Rocks but Gently* (Pye, 1967)

23

Tom Jones "Delilah" *Delilah* (Decca, 1968)

24

Monkees "Last Train to Clarksville" *The Monkees* (Colgems, 1966)
Primitives "Crash" *Lovely* (RCA, 1988)

25

Sonic Youth "Tunic (Song for Karen)" *Goo* (Geffen, 1990)
The Pixies "Bone Machine" *Surfer Rosa* (4AD, 1988)
Cocteau Twins "Lorelei" *Treasure* (4AD, 1984)
Bjork "Human Behaviour" *Debut* (One Little Independent, 1993)
my bloody valentine "Cigarette in your Bed" *You Made Me Realise* (Creation, 1988)

26

The Wedding Present "A Million Miles" *George Best* (Reception, 1987)

28

The Stone Roses "Elephant Stone" (1988, Silvertone)
The Happy Mondays "Step On" *Pills 'n' Thrills and Bellyaches* (1990, Factory)

34

Fred Waring & His Pennsylvanians "Dry Bones" (Decca, 1947)

35

The Sugarcubes "Deus" *Life's Too Good* (One Little Independent, 1988)

36

Cocteau Twins *Heaven or Las Vegas* (4AD, 1990)

39

Adam & the Ants "That Voodoo" *Prince Charming* (CBS, 1981)
Adam & the Ants "Dog Eat Dog" *Kings of the Wild Frontier* (CBS, 1980)
The Specials "Ghost Town" (2 Tone, 1981)

42

Stan Getz and João Gilberto *Getz / Gilberto* (Verve, 1964)
Bessie Smith "Need a Little Sugar in My Bowl" (Columbia, 1931)
The Sex Pistols *Never Mind the Bollocks: Here's The Sex Pistols* (Virgin, 1977)
Datblygu "Cristion yn y Kibbutz" *Wyau* (Anhrefn, 1988)
The Velvet Underground "The Gift" *White Light / White Heat* (Verve, 1968)
Barbara Streisand "Send in the Clowns" [from Stephen Sondheim's *A Little Light Music*] *The Broadway Album* (Columbia, 1985)

43

David Bowie *Low* (RCA, 1977)
New Order "Vanishing Point" *Technique* (Factory, 1989)

44

my bloody valentine "Instrumental no 2" (Creation, 1988)
my bloody valentine *Isn't Anything* (Creation, 1988)
my bloody valentine "Honey Power" & "Moon Song" *Tremolo* (Creation, 1991)

45

Adam & the Ants *Kings of the Wild Frontier* (CBS,1980)

46

Soft Cell "Tainted Love" and "Say Hello, Wave Goodbye" *Non-Stop Erotic Cabaret* (Some Bizzare, 1981)
Duran Duran "Last Chance on the Stairway" *Rio* (EMI, 1982)

47

Phil Oakey & Giorgio Moroder "Together in Electric Dreams" *Philip Oakey & Giorgio Moroder* (Virgin, 1985)

58

Lush "Sweetness and Light" *Gala* (1990, 4AD)
Ride *Going Blank Again* (Creation, 1992)
Lush "Nothing Natural" *Spooky* (4AD, 1992)
Bob Dylan "Rainy Day Women #12 + 35" *Blonde on Blonde* (Columbia, 1966)

62

Dyma'r Rysait [An Artists For Animals Compilation]:Y Gwasgwyr "Ond Mae'r Dawns yn Mynd Ymlaen", Eirin Peryglus "Cusanau'r Gwaed", Datblygu "Brechdanau Tywod", Crisialau Plastig "Rigor Mortis" (OFN, 1988)
Y Cyrff *Dan y Cownter* (Yn Fyw) (Y Cyrff, 1985)
Anhrefn *Defaid, Skateboards a Wellies* (Workers Playtime, 1987)
Traddodiad Ofnus *Welsh Tourist Bored* (Constrictor, 1987)
Ffa Coffi Pawb *Dalec Peilon* (Ankst, 1988)

63

Datblygu "Bar Hwyr" *Trosglwyddo'r Gwirionedd* (NEON, 1983)
Datblygu "Dafydd Iwan yn y Glaw" *Wyau* (Anhrefn, 1988)

Public Image Ltd. *Metal Box* (Virgin, 1979)
The Fall *Bend Sinister* (Beggars Banquet, 1986)
The Jesus and Mary Chain *Psychocandy* (Blanco y Negro, 1985)
Patti Smith *Horses* (Arista, 1975)

64

PJ Harvey "Send His Love to Me" *To Bring You My Love* (Island, 1995)

67

Madness "Shut Up" *7* (Stiff, 1981)

71

The Buggles "Video Killed the Radiostar" *The Age of Plastic* (Island, 1980)
Abba "SOS" *ABBA* (Epic, 1975)
Elvis Presley "There's a Brand New Day on the Horizon" *Roustabout* (RCA, 1964)
The Cure "Plastic Passion" *Boys Don't Cry* (Fiction, 1980)

72

David Bowie "Ziggy Stardust" *The Rise and Fall of Ziggy Stardust and the Spiders from Mars* (RCA Records, 1972)
The Fall "New Big Prinz" *I Am Kurious Oranj* (Beggars Banquet, 1988)

73

Japan "Ghosts" *Tin Drum* (Virgin,1981)
Joy Division "Love Will Tear Us Apart" (Factory, 1980)
Depeche Mode "Somebody" *Some Great Reward* (Mute, 1984)
Kylie Minogue "I Should be So Lucky" *Kylie* (PWL, 1987)

76

PJ Harvey "Sheela-Na-Gig" *Dry* (Too Pure, 1992)
Patrick McNee & Honor Blackman "Kinky Boots" (Decca, 1964)
Crumblowers *Llithro mewn i Ffantasi* (Headstun, 1989)
Y Fflaps *Amhersain* (Probe Plus, 1988)
The Slits *Cut* (Island, 1979)
Gadael yr Ugeinfed Ganrif [Compilation featuring bands Yr Anhrefn, Elfyn Presli, Datblygu, Traddodiad Ofnus, Igam Ogam] (Anhrefn, 1985)

77

Coldplay *A Rush of Blood to the Head* (Parlaphone, 2002)
PJ Harvey *Let England Shake* (Island, 2011)

Notes

1. Figures from the Welsh Revenue Authority https://gov. wales/welsh-revenue-authority

2. https://www. itv.com/news/wales/2022-07-19/second-homes-what-are-they-exactly-and-whats-the-issue